LIFE
AFTER
DEATH
AND THE
WORLD
BEYOND

LIFE AFTER DEATH AND THE WORLD BEYOND

Investigating Heaven and the Spiritual Dimension

JENNY RANDLES & PETER HOUGH

© 1996 Jenny Randles and Peter Hough

First published in 1996 by
Judy Piatkus (Publishers) Ltd
5 Windmill Street, London W1P 1HF

This edition published in 1999

The moral right of the authors has been asserted

A catalogue record for this book
is available from the British Library

ISBN 0–7499–1802–0 pbk
0–7499–1681–8 hbk

Edited by Esther Jagger
Designed by Paul Saunders
Picture research by Jennifer Hiney

Set in Goudy Old Style by
Phoenix Photosetting, Chatham, Kent
Printed and bound in Great Britain by
Butler & Tanner Ltd, Frome and London

CONTENTS

PICTURE CREDITS

Permission to use copyright photographs is gratefully acknowledged to the following: *page 8* Bibliotheque Nationale, Paris/Bridgeman Art Library; *page 9* Egyptian National Museum, Cairo/Bridgeman Art Library; *page 15* Giraudon/Bridgeman Art Library; *page 16* Mueso Diocesano, Cortona/Bridgeman Art Library; *page 18* British Library, London/Bridgeman Art Library; *page 20* Geoff Swaine/London Features International Ltd; *page 28* Tretyakov Gallery, Moscow/Bridgeman Art Library; *page 30* Michael Bromley; *page 39* Palazzo Ducale, Venice/Bridgeman Art Library; *pages 46 and 49* Peter Hough; *page 50* Lloyd Andrews/Villard Books; *page 60* Corbis-Bettman/UPI; *page 69* Peter Hough; *page 72* Mary Evans Picture Library; *pages 75 and 76* Psychic News; *page 79* Mary Evans Picture Library; *page 80* Peter Hough; *page 83* Museo Diocesano, Cortona/Bridgeman Art Library; *page 86* LWT Productions; *page 93* Hilary Evans/Mary Evans Picture Library; *page 99* Solo Syndication Ltd; *page 100* Dave Brinicombe/The Hutchinson Library; *pages 105 and 108* Hotel Dieu, Beaune/Bridgeman Art Library; *page 110* Psychic Press; *pages 111 and 112* Cassell's History/Mary Evans Picture Library; *page 120* Corbis-Bettmann/UPI; *page 122* Psychic Press (1995) Ltd; *page 123* Mary Evans Picture Library/College for Psychic Studies; *page 139* Mary Evans Picture Library/Society for Psychical Research; *page 143* Psychic Press (1995) Ltd; *page 148* Corbis-Bettmann; *page 151* Grafton Books; *page 156* Psychic Press (1995) Ltd; *page 161* Grafton Books. Whilst every effort has been made to trace all copyright holders, the publishers apologise to any holders not acknowledged.

ACKNOWLEDGEMENTS

We would like to thank the following for their cooperation and assistance: Alan Bell, Michael Bentine, Albert Budden, Andy Collins, Doris Collins, Don Henderson, Tim Haigh, Dr Moyshe Kalman, Alicia Leigh, Susie Mathis, Michael McGarvie, Professor Kenneth Ring, Joe Ritchie, Jean Rogers, Mark Simpson, Professor Alan Smithers, Hilda Totty, all the staff at *Psychic News* plus the many experients who preferred to remain anonymous.

INTRODUCTION

HEAVEN... the concept of a world beyond material existence is a staple element of the collective consciousness of the human race, and has been for thousands of years. It forms part of ancient and modern pagan beliefs, and of the Christian, Islamic, Judaic, Hindu and Buddhist religions. A spiritual plane has been central to the faiths of most ancient civilisations, including those of the Egyptians, Greeks and native Americans. In some cultures heaven was (and is) perceived as a physical, literal place, peopled with gods and goddesses who to all intents and purposes resembled humans, although they possessed supernatural powers. Other societies, arguably more sophisticated, regard heaven as a mental construct. In the modern world, even many agnostics are convinced that consciousness does not cease with physical death, but survives and passes on to another place.

Egyptian tomb painting showing the departed before Osiris, Isis, and Thoth, c 2850 BC

Why? What is the purpose of such a place, physical or imagined? Was the afterlife perhaps invented as an aid for social control? If people could be persuaded to believe in a heaven for the righteous (and, conversely, a hell for those who acted badly on earth), then crime would be less of a problem. Or is the concept of heaven just a piece of wishful thinking, designed to make the thought of the inevitability of death more palatable?

OPPOSITE PAGE A thirteenth century depiction of a good man being taken to heaven and a greedy man to hell (Hebraica Romana Gallica)

9

We need the conviction that we are more than flesh and blood – an entity independent of the physical ravages of time. We want to believe in our own immortality, that after our spell on the physical plane we are taken to a world of beauty or pleasure – perhaps to rest a while until we are reborn. But before we can be convinced of this, most people require some sort of proof.

If heaven is more than just imagination, where does this proof lie? Are near-death experiences an extension of a fantasy, or do they offer some evidence of a place which we call heaven? Do so-called past lives demonstrate the survival of consciousness outside the restrictions of time and space and, if so, where are we in the years between incarnations? Are encounters with angels and visions of the Virgin Mary evidence of psychosis, or do supernatural entities really visit us from heaven? Are those who believe in the afterlife living under a gigantic delusion, or are they responding to messages from heaven?

This book sets out to explore the possibility of heaven, in some form, existing as an objective reality, and offers various kinds of evidence for readers to assess. It contains the ultimate in travellers' tales – first-hand reports from people who have died and supposedly made that final journey. Many of these reports come by way of mediums who believe that they are a conduit between this world and the next.

Much of the information received in this way is supposedly channelled from afterlife entities and spirit guides. These guides can take temporary possession of the medium, using their vocal cords and manipulating their hands and bodies. Are such messages the product of imagination? Are they mere fraud? Or could they be genuine?

Contact with the spirit world apparently also keeps pace with modern technology. Groups in America and Europe claim to be in communication with the dead through radio, television pictures, computers and fax machines.

These messages form the latter part of the book, from Chapter 9 onwards. Preceding them are stories of people in this life who have gained a brief glimpse of what might lie beyond, perhaps through a near-death experience or an encounter with a supernatural entity, but whose time has not yet come.

Religious upbringing and beliefs acquired in adult life will colour your views on the subject, and dictate your response to the accounts in this book. Whatever your opinions on the afterlife, it will be shared by some and rejected, perhaps with hostility, by others. Nobody knows for certain the truth about life after death, and that includes members of all the major religions and scientific thought.

We, the authors, do not pretend to know the ultimate answer, and would not attempt to convince you that we do. Only you can decide if these eye-witness accounts of heaven strike a chord, or come across as delusions, distortions of the truth, or cruel, deliberate deceptions.

All that is required is a willingness to listen. What you finally believe is up to you.

Chapter 1

HEAVEN: THE TRADITIONAL VIEW

I N THE ancient civilisations and religions, heaven was traditionally the place where gods, goddesses and other spiritual beings resided. The oldest religious texts describing a belief in an afterworld are to be found on the walls of pyramids at Sakkara, Egypt, and are around four thousand years old. Native Americans pointed up to the stars and saw them as camp fires lit by their ancestors in the Happy Hunting Grounds. Australian Aborigines believe that the dead are taken up into the sky, and eventually return to earth. To such peoples, past and present, heaven exists Out There, conceived as being beyond the canopy of sky. Shooting stars and thunderbolts were interpreted as signs from the gods and reinforced this belief. Heaven was the place where the souls of those who lived their lives correctly on earth went. It was the just reward, a blissful abode, the ultimate goal – it was paradise.

Shooting stars and thunderbolts were interpreted as signs from the gods

THE GOOD PLACE

PARADISE has meant different things to different cultures, but essentially it is a Good Place reflecting whatever was deemed most desirable by a particular society in their earthly, material lives. Avalon, the Elysian Fields, Valhalla and the Garden of Eden are all examples of variations on this theme. Sometimes this Good Place was seen as existing in some distant part of the earth, and sometimes elsewhere beyond the earth. The word 'paradise' itself is of Old Persian origin, and originally meant an area of enclosed land which cultivation had made more agreeable than its surroundings – put simply, an oasis surrounded by desert.

This translates into a metaphysical garden, a place seeded and built by the will of supernatural beings, containing the most beautiful and colourful plants laid out in an aesthetically pleasing way. In less sophisticated cultures, paradise also reflected the pleasures of the flesh.

VALHALLA

THIS was the paradise of Norse mythology, ruled by the god Odin. Followers of Odin who died in battle or sacrificed themselves to the god were rewarded by being conveyed to the Hall of Valhalla. There they were greeted by the Valkyries – fierce battle-maidens – and handed horns of mead.

This is no bright place in the heavens, but a fun palace catering for the blood-lust of aristocratic warriors. In the Hall of the Slain, men fought one another all day – but those who were killed were miraculously restored in the evening to enjoy a feast of pork and mead.

Valhalla was a fun palace catering for the blood-lust of aristocratic warriors

AVALON

AFTER receiving a fatal wound, King Arthur was taken to the Celtic island paradise of Avalon. He was transported there in a boat by several fairy women. Avalon was first mentioned by the twelfth-century chronicler Geoffrey of Monmouth, who said that it was ruled over by Morgan, the fairy queen.

An earthly location for Avalon has been identified with Glastonbury in Somerset. Before monks drained the area in the Middle Ages, the hill known today as Glastonbury Tor was an island surrounded by lagoons and waterways. The Tor is steeped in myth and fairy legends, and was thought to be a portal into fairyland. Even today, strange things reportedly happen there.

Glastonbury Tor, steeped in myth and legend, was once thought to be a portal into fairyland

THE ELYSIAN FIELDS

IN Greek mythology, Elysian or the Elysian Fields was the name given to a land of happiness and perpetual spring. Those favoured by the gods lived there, exempt from death. It was ruled by Rhadamanthus, and according to the poet Homer was situated on the banks of the mythical River Oceanus at the end of the earth.

This paradise was refined by later classical writers and became part of the underworld, where only the righteous went after death. But as belief in Elysian evolved, its location was finally transferred to the sky.

The underworld *per se* was a more sinister place: Hades was nearer to hell than to heaven. It was ruled by Persephone and her husband Pluto, beautiful and powerful gods who were not exactly benign. It was to Hades that the 'shade' or psyche of a person descended. Because the underworld was a place stripped of physical pleasures, to the Homeric heroes it was an insubstantial abode of misery. The Romans blended the Greek underworld with their own myths and ideas to make it become a place of retributive punishment where the guilty were tortured by demons.

THE ISLES OF THE BLEST

THE belief in the Isles of the Blest was part of Greek culture, later also assimilated by the Romans into their mythology.

In the Isles of the Blest, dead souls spent their time feasting and making love

This place too was supposedly situated on earth, in the far west where the sun sets. Paradise existed on earth at a time when the planet itself remained largely unexplored and was as mysterious and alien as outer space. The souls of the dead went to this otherworld, which was like a beautiful garden. There they spent their time listening to music and indulging in material pursuits which included feasting and making love.

An ancient Irish seafaring tale called *The Voyage of Bran* tells of a trip to these islands, a place described as 'without grief, without sorrow, without death'. St Brendan is also said to have sailed to their shores.

THE GARDEN OF EDEN

THE biblical book of Genesis describes how God planted a paradise 'in Eden, in the east' after creating the world. Was this heaven easier for men to conceive if given a location on earth? Certainly Eden is no normal garden.

Unlike other paradises this was not a place where the dead went, but a garden where the newly created man and woman lived with the other beasts of the land and air. But Eden was without death.

Adam and Eve were immortal until they disobeyed God and ate the fruit of the tree of knowledge. Then they were cast out of this heaven to toil the dust which had borne Adam – the dust to which he now would return. The only way for Adam and Eve to regain their immortality was to eat from the tree of life. God ensured that they could not do so by placing an angel with a flaming sword outside Eden to guard the entrance.

As a result of this misbehaviour in the Garden of Eden, Christians see mankind as a fallen race. Every child is born with the stigma of original sin, and baptism is used to cleanse the soul. In traditional Christian belief there are three possible destinations for the dead; heaven, purgatory or hell.

Sinners were cast into three categories. Those whose sins could be forgiven on earth, those with more serious misdemeanours which had to be purged in purgatory, and those sinners who were beyond redemption and suffered for all time in hell.

Those who had reached heaven were perceived gloating from on high, watching those below suffering fiery tortures

Purgatory is viewed as a way-station between this world and heaven. In the *Aeneid*, Virgil pictured a trinity of purges for the tainted soul: the effects of fire, wind and water. Some were seared with flame, others hung out to be buffeted by razor sharp winds, and some suffered in a gigantic whirlpool. These punishments were to last a thousand years, at the end of which the soul was fit to enter heaven.

During the Middle Ages a horrifying picture of hell was created. Those who had reached heaven were perceived gloating from on high, watching those below suffering fiery tortures. Such scenarios could be viewed as a means of social control by the Church who at that time wielded extensive power in Europe.

RIGHT *An early fifteenth century illustration of hell (Pol de Limbourg)*

A VISION OF HEAVEN

GENESIS 28 provides us with a further glimpse of the traditional Christian view of heaven. It documents the flight of Jacob from his older brother, after he had tricked Esau out of his birth right. When night drew in he settled down, using a rock for a pillow, and went to sleep, then began dreaming.

Jacob saw a staircase reaching from the ground up towards heaven. Angels were going to and fro on the steps, and at the top stood God. God told Jacob that the place where he slept was his, and that he was to populate the land with his children.

Upon awakening, Jacob was convinced by the vision and said: 'Surely the Lord is in this place. This is the house of God and this is the gate of heaven.' Jacob named the place 'Bethel'.

This story is also a biblical example of the visionary experiences reported in this book. Although Jacob described the encounter as a 'dream', it was much more powerful and real than that. Powerful enough to change his life.

ANGELS

ALMOST every religion incorporates angels in one form or another as part of the hierarchy of heaven. The word 'angel' translates in both Hebrew and Greek as 'messenger' and comes from the Latin *angelus*. Angels are conceived of as benevolent supernatural beings and were God's first creation, formed out of fire. They feature in both the Old and New Testaments. In the Old Testament they took a more active role than mere messengers from God, and advised and helped entire nations. In Daniel 10 and 12 the 'chief prince' of angels, Michael, is described as 'the great prince who has charge of your people'.

Several Christian angels are shared with Islam, for instance Gabriel/Jabril and Michael/Mikail. Moslems have Azrail, the angel of death, while Christians have their fallen angel, Satan.

In Islam there are three kinds of angels: those who do nothing but worship Allah, those who control the forces of nature and inflict death, and the *hafaza* – guardian angels who protect individuals from djinns or demons. The classical Greek writer Menander commented: 'By every man at birth a good demon takes his stand, to initiate him in the mysteries of life.'

Menander was describing not an evil spirit, but a stern supernatural guide. Today, belief in guardian angels is stronger than at any recent time.

GIFTS FROM HEAVEN

IF we are to take Bible stories at face value, it would seem that objects, as well as beings, are able to manifest from heaven into our world. Exodus 16 describes how Moses led the Israelites from Elim into the wilderness of Sin. As their suffering increased, the people began to regret leaving Egypt. They blamed Moses, but God came to his aid, saying: 'I will rain bread down from heaven for you. The people shall go out and gather a certain amount every day, so that I may test them, to see whether they will obey my laws. And it shall be arranged that on the sixth day they shall prepare what they bring in, which shall be twice as much as they gather on other days.'

Moses told the Israelites what God had promised, and 'the glory of the Lord appeared in a cloud'. God told Moses that in the evening they would eat meat, and in the morning they would eat bread. That evening quails appeared over the camp, and in the morning the ground was littered with flakes of bread which were given the name 'manna'.

God promised Moses: 'I will rain bread down from heaven for you'

PASSPORT TO HEAVEN

IN some cultures, living by a moral code on earth did not automatically guarantee access to heaven. Belief in judgement is widespread and very ancient. It is first mentioned in Egyptian records dated around 2400 BC. The Egyptians, and later the Jews, taught that the soul was judged by the deity before a final decision was made.

The Jews developed a belief in the Last Judgement, which was taken over by Christianity. At the end of the world everyone who has ever lived is to be resurrected so they can be judged by God. Those who have sinned against God sink into the pit of hell, and others live a life of pleasure in paradise.

In Islam the dead are interrogated by two angels who expect them to have a full knowledge of their religion. If they answer correctly, a door to heaven opens but if their answers are wrong they enter the pit of hell. The Koran describes heaven as an oasis of gardens, rivers and trees where men wined, dined and enjoyed the pleasures of harems. Moslems now believe, however, that heaven is where God is – a place of pure goodness.

These two very different interpretations of heaven are explained in terms of Moslem society at different cultural periods. In ancient times a

The ascent of the prophet Muhammad to heaven (Aqa Mirak, 16th century). This painting shows the traditional Islamic concept of heaven

desert-dwelling people would envisage paradise as a green cool oasis as opposed to the dry sands and burning winds of their natural environment. With the spread of Islam beyond the inhospitable regions of the world, 'a place of pure goodness' would act as a balance against western materialistic obsession.

Buddhism, which grew out of Hinduism in the sixth century BC, devised a series of graded paradises, each more sensual and beautiful than the last. Ascent depended on individual virtue and meditation. Heaven for Buddhists and Hindus is release from the bondage of personality into a pure spiritual state which they call nirvana. This transformation is a final release from the cycle of reincarnation.

HERE AND NOW

What bearing do traditional views of heaven have on the here and now? Do they equate with the descriptions of today's experients who believe they have glimpsed the afterworld?

In the past so much was accepted on faith. Now, in the dying years of the twentieth century, we demand a more critical look at such claims, and ask whether heaven does indeed exist as a 'place', or whether it lies solely in the imagination.

Chapter 2

WARNINGS OF DEPARTURE

I F DEATH is meaningless, pointless, a trip to nowhere, why would acquaintances, close friends and relatives receive advance news of the departure of a loved one? If we are mere biological machines fit only for recycling at the end of our shelf life, how could we be capable of communing on a psychic level with the dead and dying? The following cases demonstrate beyond reasonable doubt that this does indeed occur. The ramifications could point towards proof in our search for heaven.

Actor Brian Blessed, pictured below with his wife, sensed the unexpected death of his mother-in-law whilst filming abroad

SENSATIONS OF PASSING

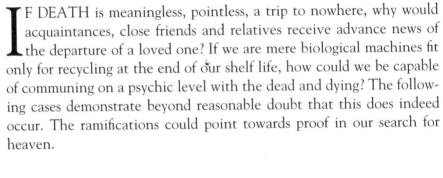

How is it that those who are alive can sometimes sense the passing of others? Social security fraud inspector Kevin McClure described how he was overcome by a wave of depression and foreboding, so out of keeping with his previous state of mind, that he remained sleepless far into the night. Kevin was still wide awake when the police called to advise him to travel the hundred miles to London, where his grandfather was dying.

British actor Brian Blessed told Jenny Randles of an incident which occurred when he was making a film in a foreign country. As he rehearsed a scene, a sudden depression surged through him. He told some of the other actors present, who included Kenneth Branagh,

that he felt as if his mother-in-law, Josie Zimmerman, was calling out to him. A telephone call to England revealed that Josie had suffered a fatal heart attack at the same time that he experienced his strange sensation.

Another British actor, Don Henderson, was making his TV series *Bulman* in 1985 when he had a devastating experience. He was filming the final scene of an episode entitled 'Sins of Omission' with his co-star, an actor called George Pravda, who played Pushkin, a KGB agent. Bulman was meant to pay an emotional farewell to Pushkin, who was due to return to the USSR. In fact Henderson knew that the character was to return in a future series.

The script called for Bulman to hug Pushkin and whisper in Russian, 'Goodbye, old friend.' As the scene was filmed, Henderson felt himself swamped with pain and grief; he really felt that he was never going to see George again. Afterwards, the director congratulated Don on his outstanding performance. But the actor knew that the emotions he had displayed to the camera were real. A few weeks later George Pravda died quite unexpectedly of a heart attack.

Swamped with pain and grief, Don Henderson felt he was never going to see his friend again

DREAMS

MANY warnings of death go beyond feelings to involve visual premonitions – in the form of dreams.

Reach out

Eileen Harris lives at White Rock, Nova Scotia in Canada. She has an arts degree, majoring in music, and taught in a large school before she was married. She told us: 'I am not the sort of person who accepts uncanny happenings without question, and I never expected anything "strange" to happen to me.' Nevertheless, something strange did happen.

Eileen grew up in a rural community where everyone knew everyone else. Amongst her childhood friends were the three daughters of the Harveys, who ran the local post office and general store. The Harvey children gradually grew up and moved away; Eileen married within the community and, despite the age difference, befriended the Harvey parents. During the 1960s the Harveys gave up their business as they could not compete with the new supermarkets in nearby towns.

Mr Harvey was in any case not in the best of health after suffering a slight stroke, so they decided to move into a senior citizens' complex in

Berwick, about twenty-five miles away. Eileen then more or less lost touch with them.

'At the time of my "odd experience" they had been living in Berwick for several years, and I hadn't consciously thought of them in recent months at all. None of our neighbours had happened to mention them, and I had plenty on my plate to think about.' Apart from two children, Eileen had to care for grandparents and her husband, who had suffered an industrial accident.

'One morning I awoke after experiencing a very vivid dream in which Mr Harvey was lying on a hospital bed, and his wife was hovering over him in a state of great agitation and concern. It was as real as could be, and her worried state came through very clearly. I sat up in bed and said aloud, "Mr Harvey is dying, or perhaps he is already dead!"

'The dream haunted me all morning. Finally I phoned a close friend who was related to the Harveys, and asked if they had heard anything from the couple recently. I didn't mention my strange dream. "Odd that you should ask me that today," said my friend. "John" – one of the Harveys' sons – "just left here a short time ago. He got an urgent call from Berwick this morning. His father had a very severe stroke in the night. They don't think he will last long."'

Mr Harvey died not long afterwards. Eileen wonders if her elderly friend was telepathically reaching out to her when his life was almost over.

Late arrival

Lee Fields has had several precognitions. In early February 1981 she and her soldier husband of one month moved to Germany, where he was to do a tour of duty. They had only been there about a week when Lee had a strange dream after her husband had got up early, leaving her asleep.

She was driving along a familiar road in her native Liverpool. On the pavement she saw one of her brothers, dressed in a black suit and gazing at her as if she was in a funeral procession. Next to him was her father. He was wearing a plain grey suit and stood firm, as if to attention, with a deadpan expression on his face.

Lee pulled up beside the two men and got out of the car. 'James,' she said, 'what's wrong with Dad?' There was no reply. Next she turned to her father and spoke to him. His reaction was to crumple to his knees and grasp her tightly around the waist, sobbing.

When she woke up she toyed with the idea of telephoning home, but decided not to, trying to convince herself it was 'only' a dream. There

On the pavement she saw her brother, dressed in a black suit and gazing at her as if she was in a funeral procession

was a special bond between father and daughter, as she was the only girl in the family. So when the news came, it hit especially hard.

The family had not notified her immediately in case their alarm was premature. Her father had been rushed to hospital on the same morning that Lee had the strange dream. She flew back to England to be greeted by her brother's stony expression, just as she had seen it in the dream. Her father had begun his journey beyond the veil before her arrival. If she had trusted her dream and telephoned immediately, Lee might have arrived in time to see him before he died.

APPARITIONS IN CRISIS

SOMETIMES people actually 'see' the dying or newly deceased as part of their waking environment. There are many accounts of apparitions appearing at the moment of death; they are referred to as 'crisis apparitions'. At this time it seems that a part of us can be projected towards a relative or close friend. This can even happen to people who later recover. It is not death itself which is the mechanism, but a belief in impending doom.

At the moment of death it seems that a part of us can be projected towards a relative or close friend

The figure in the washroom

Winnie Pianko, a warden in a Herefordshire nursing home, was working alone one night. Wanting to visit the toilet, for some unknown reason she did not cross the corridor to the nearest one, but took the much longer route to a toilet downstairs. As she entered she was confronted by 'a young man in a grey suit'. Thinking he was an intruder, she asked him what he was doing. He replied: 'Tell Mam not to worry.' Then he vanished.

Winnie knew that she recognised the man, but could not place him. The following day, as she waited for a bus, she overheard a conversation about the death of a local man the night before. She knew him slightly, as he was a distant relative. Winnie realised that it was his apparition which she had seen in the washroom. Now she could convey his message of survival to his grieving family.

Accident at sea

The Society for Psychical Research (SPR) was founded in 1882. Amongst its early members were scientists like Sir William Barrett, Sir Oliver Lodge and Sir Alister Hardy. The society seeks to examine psychic experiences in an unbiased and scientific way. One of the earliest cases the SPR recorded was an account by a Mrs Collyer, who on 3 January 1856 went to bed early because she was unwell. Some time later she felt uneasy and sat up in bed. She was amazed to see standing in the room her son Joseph, who she thought was at sea.

'He was looking at me with great earnestness, his head bandaged, a dirty nightcap on, and a dirty white garment on, something like a surplice. He was much disfigured about the eyes and face.'

Mrs Collyer's fears were confirmed when on 16 January she learned of Joseph's death. She had seen him at the moment of his death, which was the result of a collision. The details of the clothes he was wearing and the injuries he sustained were subsequently confirmed by his shipmates.

Down to earth

The SPR cite the following case as amongst the most impressive of some hundred similar reports. Here, the percipient described the experience to a colleague, who verified that it happened before anyone realised that the figure was not a flesh-and-blood man. The account was written down shortly after the event.

On the morning of 7 December 1918, eighteen-year-old trainee pilot Lieutenant David McConnel was asked to fly a Camel aircraft to Tadcaster in Yorkshire. He was based at Scampton in Lincolnshire, sixty miles from his destination. At 11.30 a.m. he took leave of his room-mate, Lieutenant Larkin, saying he expected to be back for tea.

Several hours after McConnel had departed, Larkin was reading and smoking in his room when he heard someone walking along the passage. The door then opened with the noise and clatter that McConnel always made, and Larkin heard him say, 'Hello, old boy!'

Lieutenant Larkin turned round in his chair and saw McConnel standing in the doorway with his hand on the knob. He was dressed in full flying outfit but wearing his naval cap, which was rather odd. The two exchanged a few words, after which McConnel said, 'Well, cheerio!', went out and shut the door loudly.

Larkin did not have a watch, but was certain that the time was between a quarter-past and half-past three, because shortly after that a Lieutenant Garner-Smith came in and it was then a quarter to four. He enquired whether McConnel was back yet, because they had all three planned to go into Lincoln for the evening. Larkin explained that he had just seen McConnel, and Garner-Smith went in search of the trainee pilot.

He never found him, so the pair went to Lincoln on their own. While they were having a drink in the Albion Hotel they overheard a group of officers discussing a plane crash and the death of the pilot – Lieutenant McConnel.

The violence of the crash had stopped the pilot's watch at 3.25am

Apparently when he arrived at Tadcaster the aerodrome had been shrouded in dense fog. He had lost control of the Camel, which had nose-dived and crashed. The violence of the impact had stopped his watch at 3.25 p.m.

Sceptical investigator Dr West was impressed by the well-corroborated case: 'There are few others in the SPR collection which reach the same standard.' He argued that in most cases the apparition is seen as a mute figure, but here it appeared completely life-like, seemed to interact with its environment and held a conversation with a human being. Yet why it did not report its death to Lieutenant Larkin is a mystery.

Did Larkin have a hallucination? He was expecting McConnel back for tea, so did he imagine his return? The investigators found no evidence that any similar 'hallucinations' had been experienced by Lieutenant Larkin, who stated that for him the occasion was quite exceptional.

Final act

Anna, from Switzerland, was attending a horticultural college in England in 1936 when she befriended a girl called Patricia. There was another Swiss student, Trudy, there with Anna, and at first Patricia acted in a reserved manner towards them as they were foreigners. But the three girls' mutual love of animals and plants drew them closely together.

Two years later, back in Zurich, Anna met Trudy at midday on 14 February. Suddenly, Anna caught sight of their English friend walking through the crowds. Despite the warm weather Patricia was wearing her old raincoat and hat. Anna told Trudy that she had spotted Pat and ran across to speak to her.

'Pat was just getting into a No. 5 tram. I saw her take her seat, but before I could reach the tram it started off.'

But Trudy had not seen Pat. Some days later Anna received a letter from Pat's mother, which said that her daughter had been killed in an accident. Pat had been thrown from her horse and broken her neck at midday on 14 February.

SAYING GOODBYE

THESE experiences demonstrate something truly paranormal. The percipients could not have known in the 'normal' way what had happened to their friends and loved ones. The possibility of chance is so remote that it can be ignored. Some kind of communication occurs which is either a natural process, or purposely instigated by the deceased or some greater power.

However, the choice of percipient often seems arbitrary. Why did Pat appear to her school friend and not to her mother, with whom one might assume she had a stronger emotional bond? Eileen Harris saw Mr Harvey dying in a dream. Why Mrs Harris, whom he had not seen for some time, instead of his son John? Winnie Pianko hardly knew the man whom she saw in the nursing home.

Is the answer that, when the dying are psychically reaching out, their nearest and dearest are not necessarily capable of receiving the message? They might not be 'psychic'. When this happens, second- or third-best will do. Perhaps this 'reaching out' is not focused at all, but a scatter-gun effect, where some of the pellets find their mark but most strike nothing. Nevertheless, it is as if the dead want to say goodbye before starting a journey to a foreign land, a new realm of existence.

Chapter 3

ASTRAL TRAVELLERS TO OTHER WORLDS

WHILE SOME people receive messages and see apparitions from other realms, there are others who claim they have actually left their body and ultimately travelled to other worlds. In some cases this is due to what is known as a near-death experience (NDE – see Chapter 4). The first stage in the near-death experience is often a sensation of leaving the body and this stage can occur on its own, without developing into a full-blown NDE. This is known as an out-of-body experience or OOBE. During an OOBE the percipient describes how their phantom or 'astral' body leaves their physical body.

THE ASTRAL BODY

THERE does seem to be a part of us – an essence – which is capable of survival outside of flesh and bone. It is variously described as the spirit, soul or ego. The ancient Egyptians called it *ka* and *ba*, the Greeks *psyche* and *nous*, the Moslems *sirr*, *ruh* and *nafs*, the Hindus *atman* and *jiva*, the Jews the *neshamah*, *ruah* and *nefesh*, and medieval scholars *anima divina* and *anima humana*.

The idea of the astral body provides us with an easily understood term. It is thought to be a non-material replica of the physical body. In the waking state the two bodies are in perfect alignment. Drugs, illness and extremes of age can cause the astral body to become out of 'coincidence'. There are cases on record of people going about their daily life,

> *The astral body is thought to be a non-material replica of the physical body*

Over the Town (Marc Chagall, 1887-1985). During sleep our astral body is believed to leave our physical body and travel the world

then suddenly, fleetingly, leaving their body, and finally popping back inside again. During sleep this happens naturally.

It is believed that we need to sleep because our astral body is craving release from the physical. Normally, the experience is garbled by the brain and all we remember, if anything, are the tattered remnants of 'dreams'. A dream about 'flying' is an overt memory of an actual event, according to practitioners. During this out-of-body state the astral body can travel about our world or enter another dimension known as the astral plane. This is known as 'astral travelling'.

THE VIEW FROM THE CEILING

ONE of the most remarkable accounts involves a girl called Ami from Gillingham in Kent. In 1993, at the age of three, she had already 'died' a dozen times and experienced frequent OOBEs as a result.

Ami has a rare brain disorder which affects children up to four years of age. It causes them to fall unconscious at the least shock and appear lifeless for a minute or so, after which they fully recover. What astonished Ami's parents was when their daughter described going out of her body during the seizures. She was later able to describe in detail the attempts to revive her, including whole lines of conversation, as if seen from a position up near the ceiling.

Sceptics argue that the experience is wholly created in the brain. It is able, they claim, to create a plan view of the location, just as modern computers are able to rotate images and create a three-dimensional effect from the raw data previously fed into them. But this does not explain how experients are later able to describe conversations, and even visual events that they were obviously unable to see in the normal way.

Jenny Randles investigated the case of a five-year-old boy who had a plastic valve fitted into his heart in a Merseyside hospital. On recovery, he innocently asked his mother why the doctors ignored him as he tried to talk to them during surgery. He was, he insisted, floating up by the ceiling watching the procedure. He described the valve which was being inserted into his body, even though he had never actually seen it. The theatre nurse confirmed that the boy's description was accurate.

Some people believe that in an out-of-body state they have visited other worlds and met strange beings. A few claim they can induce OOBEs. Yet this is nothing new.

Three-year-old Ami accurately described the attempts to revive her, as if she had seen them from the ceiling

SHAMANISM

THIS ancient religious phenomenon originated in Siberia, then spread to Asia and into the American continent. A shaman was a healer and priest who looked after the spiritual welfare of the tribe. These figures were seldom appointed by other tribesmen, but attained their powerful position through heredity or personal vocation. A typical candidate would have healing powers and visionary experiences; along with this frequently went a preference for solitude and a propensity to suffer fits which resulted in unconsciousness.

While such behaviour in the conventional modern Western world would be deemed anti-social or the product of mental illness, in these tribal cultures the shaman was revered. During initiation the shaman's soul was believed to be carried away by spirits, and returned once he was cured. Many authorities have sought to explain the phenomenon as a psychological disorder, but the afflicted person only became a shaman *after* his psychic crisis was resolved.

During ecstasy, the shaman's soul left his body and took part in an adventure involving torture and rebirth

In some cultures the initiatory ritual included a journey to heaven by climbing to the top of a tree. During ecstasy, his soul would leave the body and take part in an adventure involving torture and rebirth. It has always been part of the shaman's role to escort the souls of the dead to other worlds, as well as interceding on behalf of those still on earth and obtaining healing for them.

The dream walker

In recent years there has been a rise in the number of Western shamans. Although they retain many of the old cultural elements, some of the more bizarre traits have been abandoned.

Michael Bromley is a Celtic shaman who spent seven years studying with Cheyenne, Lakota, Potawatomi and Chumash native American medicine men. He told us how his work involved leaving the body and travelling on the 'astral plane'. 'I astral travel to facilitate healing and to help those near death and dying. I escort the dead to the spirit world. At other times I astral travel with the spirits of the birds and animals. There is a great feeling of freedom and light during this experience.'

When people ask Michael for assistance he never explains to them his method for carrying out healing and bringing comfort to the dying. If he did, he believes, they would not be able to cope with the idea. 'To do my work I have to enter their dreams. This is called "dream walking". However, I can't do this without their permission. This permission might be given on a subconscious level. People have said to me afterwards, "I felt you in my dreams".

'The key in bringing about healing is to work on the spirit. To do this I have to remain detached, unemotional. If I became emotionally involved my ability would be affected.'

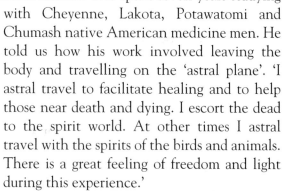

Celtic shaman Michael Bromley who astral travels 'to facilitate healing and to help those near death and dying'

ADVENTURES ON THE ASTRAL PLANE

SEVERAL years ago Peter Hough interviewed Stanley Melling, who described many of his strange journeys and encounters with other-world entities on the 'astral plane'. At the time Mr Melling was a healthy, alert sixty-eight-year-old.

Ghostly encounters

His experiences began in the summer of 1980 when he was eating lunch in his front room, staring out through the window. Opposite lived an elderly lady who had meals brought by the local social services. He looked across the narrow road, expecting to see her standing in the bay window looking out for the delivery van. There was indeed someone there – but it was not the old lady. In her place, and staring across at him, was an apparition of his dead mother.

In place of the old lady, staring at him from the window, was an apparition of his dead mother

She stood hands on hips, rigid like a statue, wearing a shawl which in life had been her favourite. Unbelieving, Mr Melling moved closer to the window until fear overcame him and he turned his head away. Then, slowly, he looked across again, but his mother's stony expression was still staring out. The image – in broad daylight – lasted for about eight minutes. Finally she turned away and the figure shape-shifted into the familiar features of the old lady. The phenomenon occurred a second time, two weeks later, under similar circumstances.

What occurred next was the penultimate episode before a great tide of OOBE-related events washed over him. At eight one morning he was woken by his alarm clock. Suddenly he heard footsteps outside the house, and children's voices which had a familiar ring. They took him back to a scene from his own childhood: picking up lumps of coal from local pits during the 1926 General Strike.

Slowly his attention was brought back to the room. His eyes focused on a spot two foot above the bed, and the intense feeling that a 'presence' hung there came over him. Then a voice spoke in his mind. 'Yes, and you will hear them again,' it said enigmatically. 'You don't die, you know!' The voice reminded him of his mother's.

From then until November 1981 Mr Melling recorded more than twenty anomalous experiences, which usually involved an out-of-body state. Most occurred on the point of falling asleep. They often began with a tiny blue light, no bigger than a pin head, hovering about nine inches above his head. After several nights the light began to pulsate,

The light began to pulsate, expanded to the size of a pea and became multi-coloured

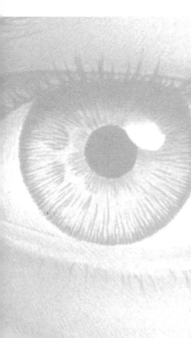

expanding to the size of a pea and becoming multi-coloured. Eventually the light would vanish, to be replaced by the vivid image of a full moon with dark clouds scudding swiftly across its surface. These clouds would thicken until only a halo remained. On these occasions Stanley Melling was drawn towards the bright ring, and through it . . . .

Through the ring

When recounting the bizarre episodes which followed his journeys through the ring, Mr Melling was at pains to convince Peter Hough of the lucidity and 'realness' of his adventures. On his first and second visits he found himself looking up a long tube or tunnel. At the other end was an eye staring down at him. On the second occasion he saw enough of the face to conclude that it belonged to a man. Mr Melling had the feeling that the man was observing him under the lens of a microscope.

Visions of the moon continued to manifest in the darkness of the room, and when the clouds obscured all but its aura, he felt himself being drawn upwards and through it. Exotic landscapes spread before him. On one journey he saw a beautiful pastoral scene of trees and flowers set around a lake. In the centre of the lake was a small rowing boat with a figure seated in it. The figure seemed to be observing Mr Melling, who in turn was observing him . . . .

Once he travelled to a barren desert strewn with rocks. A man inhabited this scene also, seated on a boulder, staring intensely in Mr Melling's direction. These figures cropped up many times in various guises. They all shared physical characteristics and behaviour – always alone, never speaking or moving, and very aware of his intrusion. Most of the men had a 'foreign' look, possibly Greek, with olive complexions, beards and short tight curly hair. There were a few exceptions. The man in the desert, for instance, wore a long robe and was completely bald.

Ringmaster of the galaxies

Mr Melling described how one night he was taken on a journey through the galaxies. One moment he was lying on his bed, then he seemed to be travelling at tremendous speed through an intense blackness. Bright spheres rushed towards him, then away into the distance. He found this highly invigorating.

Not all of these experiences occurred whilst waiting to fall asleep – sometimes he was woken up in the early hours of the morning. On seven or eight occasions, for instance, something roused him at around six o'clock.

During a few of these he saw a man dressed in glittering trousers and tails, rather like a circus ringmaster. The man would silently wave a white stick at him, as if to emphasise a point. Usually he was only clearly visible if Mr Melling covered one eye. The last vision of this nature occurred in November 1981. A gap of almost a year followed before Stanley Melling's glimpses into other worlds resumed.

Glimpses of heaven

In contrast to the elderly Mr Melling, Larry Mayer was just three years old when he had his first glimpse of 'heaven'. As a child he was a bit of a scamp, he told Peter Hough many years later, always running off and playing quietly on his own. In the 1930s there were fewer dangers for parents to worry about. At this time, Larry's family lived on the outskirts of Sheffield in Yorkshire; close by was a park.

> *As he neared the trees, he heard the most beautiful singing he had ever heard in his young life*

One particular evening Larry wandered off and found himself drawn towards the park. As he neared the trees, he heard the most beautiful singing he had ever heard in his young life. To him it sounded like the voices of angels.

Like a child of Hamelin, he followed the sound further into the park and finally sat down on a bench. The heavenly voices were above him, so he looked up into the clear starlit sky. At the spot where the singing seemed to be coming from was – nothing. It was as if a hole had been punched through the sky – a black circle of nothingness where no stars shone.

The little boy's attention was drawn back down to the bench, and he gasped. Beside him was a large glossy book, its cover decorated in the most magnificent colours. He picked it up carefully and stared at the illustration on the front. In the bottom left-hand corner was a Stone Age man. Then he stared upwards again, his face full of wonder: the object of his attentions was the full moon.

Larry put the book down and sighed. 'I'll take this home with me,' he thought, but when he looked again it had gone.

By middle-age Larry had been married many years. For some time he had been attempting through meditation to astral travel, but to no avail. Then one night in 1973, lying awake in bed beside his sleeping wife, he seemed to manage it. As he hovered above the bed, for a moment he doubted his senses. 'What an imagination I have,' he thought, and inwardly chuckled. But it felt and looked real – vividly real. If it was all a dream, then it was a remarkably detailed dream.

'What happens now?' he thought. He looked through the bedroom window and wondered if it was possible to reach the railway line a hundred yards away. No sooner had the thought formed, than he found himself drifting through the closed window as if it was not there – out through the glass into the night air.

He reached the railway line easily, stopped, looked back at the bedroom window and was troubled at how small it appeared. Larry followed the line like a balloon on the end of a piece of string.

It was exhilarating and weird. What really impressed him was how unfamiliar this landscape looked. Here was his own neighbourhood which he knew intimately, but viewed from this new perspective it was like a foreign land.

From this new perspective in mid-air, his own neighbourhood looked like a foreign land

Then something happened which broke his reverie. Up ahead, a circle of mist formed. It was the entrance to a tunnel about twenty feet long which hung in the sky at a slight cant. Drawn towards its swirling white mouth, he felt he had to get inside and see what was there. The same curiosity which had made him experiment in the first place now drove him even further.

Larry went inside and was suddenly trapped. Hundreds of hands shot out from the floor of the tunnel and gripped at his ethereal legs. One hand caught an ankle and held it tightly. He panicked and fought to escape, yet all the time in the forefront of his mind remained the desire to find out what lay at the end of the tunnel.

Then the mist cleared and he could see out of the other end. There stood the most beautiful mountain range he had ever seen in his life. A golden sun shone in a blue sky. The scene hung tantalisingly ahead of him. It would be so easy, he felt, to give up the struggle and carry on into the paradise ahead. But something told him no, not yet, not yet. ...

He fought back with renewed vigour as the disembodied hands grasped frantically to hold him. Then it was all over. One moment he was struggling for his life, the next he was back in his body, sitting up in bed, gasping for air, feeling his pyjamas sticking to his body with sweat.

The bedside light flashed on and his wife's worried face, clouded with sleep, was before him. He told her what had happened, and she made him promise not to try to leave his body again.

QUESTIONS AND SPECULATIONS

PETER Hough discussed in detail with Mr Melling and Mr Mayer the physiological and psychological effects associated with the experiences. Were these truly glimpses of supernatural beings and other worlds, or psychological tricks brought about by abnormal brain conditions? Was it just very vivid dream imagery? Mr Melling had his own thoughts on that.

'I have dreams, but these are not dreams – when I dream there are no colours, things are not clear. During these events I receive the most inexplicable panoramic views, and throughout I sense that something is feeding information into my mind. If only more people could experience it. …'

He went on to explain that he often felt he was in two places at once: the 'here' of his bedroom, and also in another reality. In this state, time seemed to be suspended and inconsequential.

Why did Mr Melling's mother feature prominently? Was he really visited by her spirit, or was it a psychological trick fulfilling a basic need? Stanley Melling is not religious and retains his objectivity about the experiences. In an attempt to find a rational explanation he approached a prominent brain specialist, but his letters were ignored.

It is interesting that many of the experiences occurred on the brink of falling asleep or upon waking up. Psychologists believe that during these periods when the brain is neither fully awake nor fully asleep – in neutral gear, as it were – some people can perceive very convincing hallucinations. These experiences, called hypnopompic and hypnagogic imagery respectively, are believed to affect between 51 and 70 per cent of the population at some time. Although the effects are generally visual or auditory, they may also involve sensations of heat, cold, smell and touch.

Temporal lobe epilepsy?

Currently there is a lot of talk amongst sceptics of temporal lobe epilepsy, which they believe can explain the whole range of paranormal experiences from UFO abductions to near-death experiences. The temporal lobes are situated at the base of the brain and behind the frontal lobes. They are the main areas for storing memory. Epilepsy is caused by electrical abnormalities in the brain. When epilepsy is focused in this region it does not manifest outwardly in convulsions, but puts the victim into an altered state of consciousness. The subjective effects of a seizure include nausea, giddiness, palpitations and distortions of memory, giving rise to perceptual illusions and sometimes followed by amnesia.

There are some obvious correlations between temporal lobe epilepsy and 'other-world' experiences, but there are just as many elements which they do not share. We have never come across any percipient, for instance, who has described feeling ill before or during their experiences.

It transpired that, just before many of his experiences, Mr Melling found himself breathing unnaturally deeply. Could he have unwittingly put himself into a trance? The heavy breathing would involve a degree of hyper-ventilation, flooding the body with oxygen and depriving the brain of sugar.

Psychological theories cannot fully account for the richly detailed and orderly pattern of other-world encounters

Psychological theories cannot fully account for the richly detailed and orderly pattern of these other-world encounters. Certainly there seems to be a state of altered consciousness involved which opens the door to paranormal experiences, but malfunctions of the brain can only produce chaos – not order.

A LINK WITH NEAR-DEATH EXPERIENCES

*T*HESE out-of-body journeys appear to be directly related to near-death experiences, which will be discussed in detail in Chapter 4. In the former, the experient is a voluntary participant who has actively encouraged the phenomenon, while the latter seem to occur spontaneously at a time of crisis. Mr Melling's bright 'ring' into which he was drawn is analogous with the 'tunnel' described by NDE experients. Mr Mayer travelled down a tunnel while in an out-of-body state, although as far as we are aware his life was not in danger. The conclusion is that these two categories are at source one and the same.

In support of this Dr Melvin Morse, an American paediatrician who has made an extensive study of childhood NDEs, includes the following case in his book written with Paul Perry, *Parting Visions*.

'Diedra' told Dr Morse of the devastating effect on her life of the death of her newborn baby. She turned her back on her six-year-old daughter and husband, spending her time sobbing at the infant's grave.

It was a warm summer's night when she had the experience. As she knelt at the graveside, Diedra suddenly went very cold. She looked around; it was not dark any more, but sunny. Then she felt herself being pulled up a tunnel of light.

At the end of the tunnel she found herself sitting on a hill watching some adults playing with several children. She knew that one of the children was her baby. After a time the vision faded back into the darkness and she was back in the cemetery.

The story does not end there. Diedra kept the experience to herself, but her daughter came up to her and said: 'Mummy, I went with you to see baby sister. She's dead now, isn't she? Next time give her a hug for me.'

Despite the best attempts of the sceptics, there are no easy answers for these experiences.

It was not dark any more, but sunny - then she felt herself being pulled up a tunnel of light

Chapter 4

NEAR-DEATH JOURNEYS

THE term 'near-death experience' (NDE) describes an apparent journey out of the body to another dimension, often described as heaven-like. Where astral travel is often a controlled state which can occur naturally during sleep, the NDE happens spontaneously, only at a time of physical and mental crisis – when a person has died or believes they are on the point of dying. Astral travellers know they will return, but those taking the near-death journey believe they are holding a one-way ticket. Most subjects meet a being bathed in light who emanates pure goodness. After they are reunited with their body they undergo a profound change of outlook on life.

This is no new phenomenon. Accounts of such experiences go back to pre-Christian times and are even recorded in the *Bardo Thodol*, and the *Tibetan Book of the Dead*, which dates from the eighth century BC. Before 1975 they were referred to as 'deathbed visions', but in that year American medic Dr Raymond Moody published his ground-breaking book *Life after Life* in which the term, 'near-death experience' was coined.

THE SCEPTIC'S VIEW

OVER the last twenty years a lot of medical research has been carried out, stirring up controversy over whether the experiences are actual or a fantasy thrown up by the dying brain. Sceptics argue that NDEs cannot be scientifically duplicated, and are therefore no more than stories. They cite major psychoses and brain malfunctions such as temporal lobe epilepsy as the cause of the hallucinations. After all, they say, the subjects are only *near* death, so some spark of consciousness must remain or else irreversible brain damage would occur.

Experients describe travelling up a dark tunnel or along a deep valley. According to scientists such as Carl Sagan this is a subconscious memory of birth. At a time of great stress – for instance when we are dying – the mind is propelled back to this vestigial memory of being forced along the birth canal towards a circle of light.

More recently, psychologist Dr Susan Blackmore has championed the theory that NDEs are hallucinations caused by oxygen starvation and drugs administered while the patient is in a critical condition. Indeed, it is generally held that a brain starved of oxygen for more than three minutes will suffer irreversible damage. Yet we hear of case after case where patients have been certified brain-dead, then fully revive – sometimes half an hour later. Dr Melvin Morse cites the case of a small boy who had been submerged underwater in a car for almost fifteen minutes, yet made a full recovery and described his visit to 'heaven'.

Descent into the Emphyrean (Hieronymus Bosch, c 1450-1516). An early depiction of a near-death experience?

*T*HE SUPPORTERS' VIEW

*S*UPPORTERS of the NDE point to independent corroboration of some aspects of the experience. For instance (as described in Chapter 3), subjects in an out-of-body state accurately describe medical procedures and repeat whole lines of conversation heard while they were 'dead' on the operating table. In this state they have travelled through walls and described events taking place in other rooms of which they had no conscious knowledge. Researchers such as Dr Raymond Moody and British psychologist Margot Grey have many cases of this kind on file.

Proponents argue that NDEs are not the product of drugs, and cite the studies of Ronald K. Siegel in the 1970s. He carried out tests on volunteers and largely failed to duplicate the various stages of NDEs. Eventually he abandoned the idea that the phenomenon was hallucinatory, produced by chemical and electrical changes to the brain, and persued other 'rational' theories.

In the 1920s tests were carried out on volunteers who were slowly starved of oxygen. This induced impaired mental and physical abilities and resulted in convulsions. NDEs, on the other hand, are orderly and tranquil – surely not something likely to be produced by a brain in chaos and on the point of extinction.

Doctors are unsure what happens during long-term comas, but they do suspect that there is enough brain activity to allow the patient to be aware of friends and relatives at the bedside. That is why visitors are encouraged to talk to patients as if they were able to hear.

In January 1996 a British patient on the point of having his life support machine switched off suddenly came round from a 'persistent vegetative state' which had lasted several months. No doctor had predicted his recovery. He claimed to have been totally aware of all that was going on around him, and had struggled to communicate but found that his body would not respond. Most people who recover from comas do so without any memories of the immediate period after the event that placed them in this condition. However, there are exceptions.

COMA PATIENTS WITH MEMORIES

Experiences of an Italian child

Eventually, the boy said, he was told he could not remain in heaven because his parents needed him back on earth

In February 1993 *Psychic News* published a report on five-year-old Pietro Volpato from Istrana in Italy, who was struck by a car and went into a coma which lasted three months. When he came round he described an experience he had had at the moment of the accident, and which can only be described as a NDE. After passing through a tunnel and coming out into the light, he said, he continued his journey into a beautiful land which he interpreted as heaven.

Young Pietro described heaven as being bright, full of sunshine and music. He met and talked with many people whose names he remembered after his recovery. His startled parents confirmed that they were long-dead family members, of whom it was unlikely that the child could have been aware. Eventually, the boy said, he was told he could not remain in heaven because his parents needed him back on earth. Reluctantly he agreed to leave, and then awoke from the coma. The case was supported by Victor Milani, a psychologist who visited Pietro in hospital.

This story, however, highlights a recurring problem. Pietro had never met his grandfather, because he had died before the boy's birth – but he did meet him in heaven! The key element in his description of this man which helped his parents identify him was that he walked with a limp. One would think that this was a defect of the body, not the soul, and conjured up an image of a heaven populated with sick and infirm people.

Spiritualists (see p. 107) suggest that those who have passed over might choose to appear in a form that is recognisable to us here on earth. The limp would enable the boy to describe accurately someone whom his parents would recognise. Perhaps it would have been simpler for the man to have said: 'I'm your granddad. Tell your mother and father when you get back.' However, the limp enabled the boy to provide proof of his encounter.

The ghettoes of heaven

Another person who apparently went to heaven while his body lay in a comatose state was Herbert Philley. After being in a car smash in Bradford, West Yorkshire, he felt himself being pulled through a tunnel towards a bright light, then into a brilliantly illuminated landscape with 'beautiful houses, huge green trees and plants, clean pavements where people of all ages strolled happily'.

Although it was difficult to judge the passage of time, Philley was convinced that he remained there throughout the period he was comatose, communing with people from previous centuries. But he said there were ghettoes in heaven too – places where disease-ridden people lived a hand-to-mouth existence, fighting over scraps of food.

Here we have the difficulty of a spiritual place which appears to include the problems of the physical world. Perhaps Philley saw heaven in this way because that was what was in his mind. It gives a whole new meaning to the saying 'Heaven is what you make it'. We shall return to this matter in Chapter 10.

There were ghettoes in heaven, places where disease-ridden people fought over scraps of food

ESCORTED TO THE LIGHT

DID Kaye, from Durban in South Africa, witness her mother's departure to heaven? Kaye was at her hospital bedside when she died. This is what she told us: 'I saw the spirit of my mother leave her body, stand for a moment or two, gaze around the huge ward, then turn to look at me – her dark blue eyes flashing like diamonds. She smiled, and was then led by two angels out of the ward. I was spellbound.' So overwhelming were these few seconds that Kaye no longer fears death.

The nurse found herself drifting down a tunnel with the dying patient, towards the light

This is a common reaction in those who have experienced deathbed encounters. Dr Margot Grey reported this next case which was related to her by a nurse who worked in a hospice. According to the nurse, she was sitting next to a woman who was drifting slowly towards death. The nurse was so absorbed in her task that she found herself drifting down a tunnel with the patient, towards the light. At that point she was told to return. She witnessed the patient disappearing into the light, then with a jolt found herself back in her body and the patient dead.

THE PRESENCE FROM HEAVEN

THIS case combines a NDE with the manifestation of a crisis apparition. Paula, now head of the English department at a high school in the north of England, was living in Ibiza with her husband and son in 1979. One day she fell down some marble steps, suffering a hairline fracture of the skull. She was rushed to hospital, where double concussion was suspected. Paula found great difficulty in mustering her thoughts because of terrible headaches. At times she was lucid; then without warning she would drift into unconsciousness.

As a child Paula had believed in God, but for the previous fourteen years she had been an agnostic. Now, in her lucid periods, she began thinking about immortality – wondering what, if anything, would happen if she died. It was a very long night in the hospital.

The following morning, against medical advice, she discharged herself and returned home. She reasoned that there was less chance of drifting into unconsciousness if she was at home moving about and doing things.

When she arrived back at the villa her husband and son were out. The headaches suddenly became almost unbearable and Paula was convinced that something terrible was about to happen, as she explained to

Peter Hough. 'I felt a compulsion to go into the bathroom and look into the mirror. I was shocked. My face was drawn and I didn't recognise it. I felt I was being forced to look into my eyes to find some answers about myself. With the belief that I was approaching death came the fear of not continuing afterwards.'

Paula experienced an urgent need to leave a few words for her family. She wrote automatically, unaware of what she had written. When it was completed, Paula heard a female voice. 'The voice was very close to my right ear, yet inside my head too. It was very calming, and said: "Have no fear. Lie down and come to me very slowly and gently." At that moment all fear lifted from me, and I wanted to follow the voice. A "going home" feeling enveloped me.'

Paula found herself travelling fast through a kaleidoscope of misty colour. The presence accompanied her. 'She knew everything about me, and talked of people whom I'd loved. As their names were mentioned I re-experienced the emotions they had aroused in me. The voice went through a series of people from childhood friends to my mother. I remember feeling a real depth of love for her.'

Finally, Paula was taken up before a magnificent white light which drew her into it, radiating a tremendous feeling. At the same time she was aware of a chorus of voices. 'It was as if they were saying that we, on earth, are really dead, and only in spirit are we alive.'

Then a male voice came from the light. It told her not to worry, as everything would be all right. Suddenly, she was back in her body and fully conscious.

'I felt so exalted. There was a God, there was continuation – I had actually seen something. I fell down in absolute amazement, then I looked at the piece of paper. It said: "When everything is over, and there's nowhere to begin, when the fight is over, and there's no room for living, lift up your soul gently, to your God."'

> 'With the belief that I was approaching death came the fear of not continuing afterwards'

> 'It was as if they were saying that we, on earth, are really dead, and only in spirit are we alive'

An unexpected presence

Paula returned to hospital for observation, and later learned of a bizarre episode which had occurred back in England at the moment she thought she was dying. 'My mother was having a lie-in that Sunday morning. Some time between 11.15 and 11.30 she saw me enter her bedroom through one of the walls and stand at the foot of her bed. She looked in amazement, and I stood there and smiled at her, then walked back out again. At that time she didn't even know I'd had an accident.' Paula has no awareness of entering her mother's room.

For some time after her experience, she felt a heightened sensitivity to life around her. On walks in the country she saw aspects of nature normally hidden from sight. She saw things on the microscopic level, with increased colour intensity. It was as if she could actually see plants and flowers growing before her eyes.

During this period Patricia was also aware of the presence, which had followed her back and now accompanied her. She asked it questions, and it answered her. Paula wondered if the presence was simply an aspect of her own consciousness, but the answers were so detailed, and so unlike 'her', that Paula became convinced she was dealing with a real objective entity. She asked it why she had had the experience, and why she had been brought back.

'I was told there was an army of light forming in the heavens to fight the forces of darkness. I was to be part of this army, but here on the physical plane. The world was nearing destruction, and the army was to intervene. I was to play some part in that.'

Today, when she talks about it, her frustration turns to tears as she struggles with the inadequacies of language to describe her feelings. 'It is impossible to put into words. Words cannot describe what happened to me. I was not the same person when I came back. It is as if I entered another existence, as if I'd been reincarnated. After that you cannot live life as you did before.'

The answers were so detailed and so unlike 'her', that Paula became convinced she was dealing with a real objective entity

On THE THRESHOLD OF DEATH

ALTHOUGH all near-death experiences share some components, no two are exactly alike. The following case which we investigated is more detailed and vivid than most.

Knocking on the side door

Ellen Robinson was twenty-two, married with two small children and living in Australia, when she had her first near-death experience. She picked up a virus which began with a throat infection, then rapidly poisoned her body until even her skin was painful when touched. When the doctor was called he injected her with drugs, and that was the last she remembered until night-time.

The experience began with Ellen going outside her Australian home to find herself standing on a cobbled street reminiscent of her native Lancashire. The street led up to a large red-brick building. At the side of the building was a dark, tunnel-like alleyway. The street finished abruptly where the darkness began, as if it was a boundary between two worlds.

On the edge of the blackness stood the figure of her father, who had died twelve months before. He held his right hand out to her, and although his lips did not move Ellen heard him speak: 'Come on, if you want to come. I know you want to come.' Ellen began crying. 'I lifted my foot to cross over into the darkness, but I knew that if I stepped over that line I wouldn't be coming back.'

Standing behind Ellen's father was her Uncle Ted; back home the two brothers were buried together. At the bottom of the alley stood a crowd of people. They were only outlined in silhouette and their features were not visible, but the crowd could obviously see her. One lady wearing a long skirt stood out. Ellen wondered who she was. 'There were about forty people present, waving and shouting my name. They wanted me to see them so I waved back, and I really wanted to go to them.' But, thinking of her children, she put her foot back down on the cobbles and said to her father: 'I want to come, but I can't. Who'll take care of Margaret and Dennis?'

She woke to find the doctor at her bedside, slapping her hand in panic

At that she woke up to find the doctor at her bedside, slapping her hand in panic and shouting: 'Ellen! Ellen! Don't you ever do that to me again! You knocked on the side door!' He meant that she had nearly died.

Her husband never discussed that day with her, and after returning to England the couple divorced. Ellen joined the Spiritualist Church and became a medium. Mediums interface with the afterlife through spirit guides, supposedly spiritually advanced individuals now in the afterlife but who once lived on earth. Most guides tend to be native Americans, Egyptians, Tibetans and members of similar cultures who on earth are strongly aware of psychic powers. Guides also act as advisers.

At the beginning of 1994 Ellen had a reading with medium Peter McDonough. Through him a 'spirit' informed her that it knew she had a desire to discover what the other side was like. Ever since her experience she had had a desperate wish to know – although that curiosity had not removed the fear of death.

Taken to the edge of the abyss

In early June 1994 Ellen suffered a pain in her abdomen. Thinking it was mild food poisoning, she did nothing. Three days later the pain subsided.

But a month later the pain returned and her temperature shot up to 103.5 degrees Fahrenheit. A bladder infection was diagnosed, and she was put on a course of antibiotics. But Ellen was concerned that it was more than an infection, and a few days later, during meditation exercises, she asked her native American guide, White Cloud, what was wrong.

'White Cloud brought back to me a memory of my son, who swallowed some chewing gum which blocked up his bowels. My guide then showed me a tube with a split in it. He was telling me that I had a bowel problem too.'

The pains grew worse, and the following day Ellen was admitted to hospital where a scan revealed that she had a perforated bowel and peritonitis had set in. Ellen was rushed to theatre for major surgery.

'When I had the operation I had three hours to live. They said the first twenty-four hours after the operation were the most crucial. When I got back to the ward I felt an irresistible wave of death washing over me. It started in the pit of my stomach and rose up. They had given me a colostomy and I didn't want to live.'

We decided to conduct an experiment: with the assistance of psychoanalyst Dr Moyshe Kalman, Ellen was hypnotically regressed to 'relive' the incident. Hypnosis has been used effectively by the police on witnesses to crime, helping them to remember details such as car number plates. The material quoted below is a combination of Ellen's conscious recollections and hypnotically enhanced 'memory' of her near-death experience.

Near-death experient, Ellen Robinson, holding a picture of her Native American guide, 'White Cloud'

During regression subjects talk in the present, as if the experience is happening for the first time at that moment.

An interesting experiment

Once regressed, Ellen found herself standing in a garden. She was wearing a long pink and white housecoat similar to one that she owned. The garden was set on a vast plateau and surrounded by a tall hedge which continued as far as the eye could see. Between flower beds ran long, straight paths, reminding Ellen of a modern cemetery.

'It's the most beautiful garden I have ever seen. The grass isn't just green, it's a rich luminous velvety green, with not one blade out of place. Somehow I can see each and every blade. In the hedge grow large rose-like flowers. I want a closer look of those flowers. The hedge zoomed in, as if I was looking through a camera. I don't know if the hedge came to me or I went to the hedge. It was so far away.' The flowers were blood red, flame orange and sun yellow, and their petals glowed like coloured tissue paper lit from behind.

Then Ellen's father came for her, dressed in his usual waistcoat and trousers, and led her along the path towards a small gathering of people. It included the woman with the long skirt from her near-death experience in Australia. She walked with great dignity, and now Ellen recognised her from photographs: it was her great-grandmother.

> 'She tells me she's the head, the boss. She's proving to me that we reincarnate'

'She's talking to me but her mouth doesn't move. They brought me here because they know it's one of my favourite places, although I've never been here before. She tells me she's the head, the boss. She's proving to me that we reincarnate. Everyone has to come back, she says. Her husband has come back. My great-grandmother tells me I'm here to learn.'

Ellen then made a curious statement. 'My family are protecting me all around. There's a danger, but I don't know what it is.'

As they slowly walked, Ellen recognised more dead relatives. She met Uncle Ted, Auntie Annie, Auntie Sally and several other aunts. There was a surprise, too – in fact two surprises.

'A three-year-old girl has taken my left hand. She has beautiful long dark wavy hair and is wearing a navy blue dress with a white collar and little red bow. She is so like my daughter, and I recognised her instantly. My daughter miscarried three years before. This was the granddaughter I never had.

'At the side of my great-grandmother, hopping, skipping and so excited, is a little boy aged about seven. The boy's got blond hair parted down one side, grey trousers and a jumper. He was also a miscarried child, belonging to a family friend. Now, he said, he had chosen me as his grandmother. He will return to me on earth as my grandson in two years' time.'

Was this heaven?

Still under hypnosis, Ellen was asked how the garden was illuminated – could she see the sun? She said everywhere was just bright. The light came from the sky, and there was no sun visible. She said the place was so wondrous that she did not want to leave. But was this heaven? Her answer was unexpected.

'The garden's a meeting-place. It's where we have the experience.'

If it was just a meeting-place, where did the spirits go when they were not escorting a visitor around the garden?

'They go back. They just go back – they didn't tell me where.'

Out of hypnosis, Ellen was at pains to convince us of the reality of the trip.

'My spirit granddaughter's hand felt just as solid as my seven-year-old granddaughter's here on earth. It's something I'll never ever forget – her little fingers in my hand. I actually held the hand of a spirit.'

How did Ellen's hypnotic voyage compare with the original visit?

'I could virtually see it all again. It didn't have the same crystal clarity, and I didn't get the same emotional feeling. There was such a great feeling of love when I was there. I really didn't want to leave!'

'My spirit grand-daughter's hand felt just as solid as my seven-year-old grand-daughter's here on earth'

The native American medicine man

Ellen has no idea how long she was in the garden, but one moment she was there and the next back in her hospital bed. As she lay looking through the windows, darkness began to descend rapidly. Across from her she could see the three other patients in their beds. 'It's night-time,' she thought, then noticed something very strange.

'As I looked at the foot of my bed I saw clouds rolling in from either side. When they met I could no longer see the other patients or the ward. Suddenly they cleared, presenting a new scene to me, more vivid than my normal eyesight would allow.'

In the clearing stood a wigwam. Before it was a fire made of sticks which burned and smoked convincingly. Then, to the right of the fire, appeared Ellen's native American guide, White Cloud. 'When the mist rolled in I wasn't even thinking of him. It was such a surprise. I tried to sit up to see more, but there were tubes plugged into my body and I could hardly move.'

A medicine man appeared who began dancing around the fire, chanting and rattling a shaker. Ellen tried to raise herself again, and saw his moccasin-clad feet. Then White Cloud stepped forward and with his right hand touched her gently on the chest, pushing her back on to the bed.

'As I talk about it I can still feel him touching me. Then he said: "Lie still and take the healing." I lay back and the whole of my bed was lit up inside a luminous glass bubble.'

Native American guide, 'White Cloud'

According to Ellen, her recovery was rapid. The following day the nurses removed the tubes from her, and she was released from hospital a week later. 'When I had the operation I was dying. Nine days later I was home. That's incredible. No one could believe it. An operation of this order can mean up to five weeks in hospital.'

Heaven lends a helping hand

Ellen's colostomy was successfully reversed a little later. 'When I see "spirit" it takes the form of a bubble, like the soap bubbles that children blow. As Mr Mossley, the surgeon, was discussing the operation with me I saw a silver bubble from the corner of my eye.'

Ellen watched the bubble float towards the surgeon and disappear into his abdomen. She expected the bubble to reappear, but it remained inside him. Mr Mossley remained totally unaware of all this.

While in bed awaiting the operation, Ellen asked her spirit what the significance of the bubble was. She was informed that it was to reassure her and demonstrate that a spirit was with the surgeon and nothing would go wrong. The day after the operation Mr Mossley came into her room to see her. 'He apologised for the discomfort, and said it was the most difficult reverse operation he had ever done. That was why a spirit was with him – they knew how bad it was going to be!'

THE MOST AMAZING CASE OF ALL?

MANY experients are told by the Being of Light that their return to earth is for a specific purpose. On 17 September 1975, twenty-five-year-old Dannion Brinkley was talking to a friend on the telephone while a thunderstorm was gathering over his home in Aiken, South Carolina. Suddenly electricity coursed through his body, welding his shoes to the nails in the floor. Dannion was wrenched free of them and held against the ceiling in a grip of excruciating pain.

Suddenly the pain was gone and he was bathed 'in a glorious calmness'. He rolled over and saw that he was suspended in the air above his smouldering body. The young man watched as his wife fought to resuscitate him. Suddenly he was back in his body staring up at her. Ten minutes later she was joined by his friend. Dannion left his body once more and accompanied the three of them in an ambulance to hospital. On the way a tunnel formed in the air and he travelled down it towards a circle of light.

He was met by a Being of Light which bathed him in love. There were other Beings too. Dannion started experiencing episodes from his life, a so-called life review which in his case was mostly unpleasant. He experienced how other people had felt at the receiving end of his anger and bullying, and for the first time felt ashamed. Then the vibration of his ethereal body changed, and he and the Being began moving upwards through fields of energy that resembled lakes and streams.

The city in heaven

They entered what Dannion describes as 'a city of cathedrals... a monument to the glory of God'. The buildings themselves were composed of glass bricks which shone brightly from within. Dannion could feel power pulsating from the city, and knew instinctively that it was a place of learning. He was there to be instructed.

After entering one of the crystalline structures Dannion found himself alone. It was filled with benches set before a podium and everything glowed with a radiant light. Suddenly the space behind the podium was filled with thirteen Beings of Light.

Dannion only had to think of a question and he was bathed in knowledge. Then one at a time the beings approached him, each carrying a box. As each stood before him his box opened, revealing moving scenes of what was yet to happen in the world. Afterwards Dannion recorded 117 events that he had witnessed in the boxes. He claims that 95 of them took place between then and 1993.

It is easy in retrospect to claim that certain historical events were predicted, but leading NDE researcher Dr Raymond Moody claims that Dannion confided these precognitions to him in advance of their occurring. They included Ronald Reagan's presidency of the USA, the Chernobyl disaster, the break-up of the Soviet Union and the Middle East conflict.

He also predicted that in 1992 a secret alliance was to be made between China, Saudi Arabia and Syria to destroy the West's economy – principally that of the USA. He said that in 1995 a nuclear accident would poison the waters around a landmass reminiscent of Norway. A war between Russia and China and other natural and unnatural catastrophes have also been predicted by Dannion Brinkley. There was a disclaimer, however: the Beings told him that these events were not inscribed in stone, but could be avoided if humans changed their ways. At the time of writing, none of the above events has occurred.

> *The thirteenth Being of Light told Dannion that his purpose on earth was to create centres where people could reduce stress*

The thirteenth Being told Dannion that his purpose on earth was to help change people's attitudes by creating centres where people could come to reduce stress. He was then shown a vision of seven rooms, each representing a different stage in the process. Dannion was to build the equipment. The knowledge which would enable him to do so would be given to him back on earth.

In the hospital, the doctors had pronounced him dead. There was no sign of brain activity, so they wheeled him out into the corridor. Dannion found himself hovering over his lifeless body when two orderlies emerged to take it away. He had been dead for around twenty minutes.

His friend appeared in the corridor and at this point Dannion found himself back in his body, staring up at the sheet covering him. Pain hit him, and he found he could not move a muscle. Then he breathed out on to the sheet, and from that movement they saw that he was alive.

Dead again

Both internally and externally his body was wrecked. It was a long, slow, painful journey to recovery, and even then the damage to his heart caused frequent blackouts. Fourteen years later, in May 1989, it resulted in a heart attack; he then died for the second time and again left his body.

At the end of the tunnel he was met once more by the Being of Light. The second life review was much better than the first, because he had done so much good since being hit by the lightning bolt in 1975. This time he visited some majestic flowers beneath a large greenhouse, which were attended to by other Beings. These were not Beings of Light, but more like 'radiant earthlings'. Dannion found the whole atmosphere 'tremendously relaxing'. This, the Being of Light told him, was the feeling he had to achieve in the centres – and that was why he had to return.

PSYCHIC GIFTS FROM THE AFTERLIFE

MANY NDE experients claim heightened powers of sensory awareness, as we saw with Ellen Robinson and Paula. These powers often cross the line into the realms of the paranormal. We have noted this too with UFO abductees, causing us to speculate that all other-world encounters are linked in some fundamental way.

In his 1992 book *Transformed by the Light*, Dr Melvin Morse details a psychological study of hundreds of witnesses. He found they had a four times higher than average number of verifiable psychic experiences.

Dannion Brinkley discovered that he could read minds in a very spectacular way: touching a person would make whole scenes from that person's life flash before his eyes. These were key emotional scenarios that were eating away at that person. After receiving this intimate knowledge. Dannion was often able to discuss their problems with them, and go some way towards resolving these issues. Dr Moody was present at many of these impromptu demonstrations and has no doubts about their authenticity.

Touching a person would make scenes from that person's life flash before his eyes

CONCLUSIVE PROOF?

DR Peter Fenwick is a consultant neurophysiologist at St Thomas's Hospital and the Royal Maudsley Hospital in London, and President of the British branch of IANDS – the International Association for Near-Death Studies. He has an impressive track record for his empirical research into consciousness. In recent years he has searched for scientific corroboration of near-death experiences. Peter Hough interviewed him in 1990, but since then his work has taken a giant step forward.

Parallel experiments have been instigated in Britain and the Netherland headed by Dr Fenwick and Dr Pim van Lommel, senior cardiologist at the Rynstate Hospital in Arnhem. A concerted programme of NDE studies has been carried out at ten hospitals. Previously experiments were often only interviewed years after the event; now the team decided to put investigations on a scientific footing by interviewing potential experients as soon as possible after undergoing a near-death crisis.

The group that the teams chose were cardiac patients, firstly because very few drugs are used on such people, and secondly – and perhaps more importantly – their clinical death can be accurately timed and monitored by electrocardiographs. The team decided that all patients admitted to the cardiac arrest unit should be interviewed. Altogether 345 patients were included in the study. Out of these, 62 – 49 men and 13 women – reported a NDE. Of these, 35 recalled a full-blown NDE including all the main elements: a feeling of calmness and peace, watching resuscitation attempts from above, entering a tunnel, meeting a Being of Light, seeing dead relatives and friends, and reluctantly agreeing to return. The team also discovered that the length of time a patient spent dead did not correspond with the apparent passage of time during the NDE – a different timescale seemed to operate.

Approximately one year after the first interview, all the patients were contacted again. A further eighteen now admitted that they too had had a NDE but had denied it at the time for various reasons.

A unique aspect of the study sought independent proof that the self actually leaves the body. In each of the hospitals an object was placed near the ceiling of the resuscitation unit. Only one member of the team knew what the object was, or where exactly it was placed. It was frequently moved around. The researchers wanted to discover if any of the experients recollected seeing the object in their out-of-body state.

At the time of writing Dr van Lommel and Dr Fenwick were not

NDEs can be experienced by atheists or followers of any religion, introverts and extroverts

ready to disclose the results of this experiment. However, both doctors are convinced that there is 'no physical, physiological or medical explanation'. NDEs can be experienced by atheists or followers of any religion, introverts and extroverts. This accords with the research of other specialists such as Dr Michael Sabom based in Atlanta, Georgia.

BLIND FROM BIRTH TO NEAR-DEATH

SCEPTICS such as Dr Susan Blackmore argue that if NDEs really are objective experiences, and not fantasies wholly conjured up through imagery stored in the brain, there should be some cases involving experients blind from birth. On this important point Peter Hough corresponded with Kenneth Ring, Professor of Psychology at the University of Connecticut and author of several significant books. His reply was highly intriguing:

> In February 1994, a graduate student, Sharon Cooper, and I, began seeking cases by making contact with a dozen organisations for the blind in the United States. Since that time we have interviewed more than thirty respondents, almost half blind from birth, most of the rest adventitiously blind. Our findings are very clear and can be summarised as follows:
>
> 1. Blind persons report NDEs which are virtually identical to those of sighted persons.
> 2. The blind – even those blind from birth – routinely claim that they can *see* during their NDEs, both things of this world and things of an otherworldly nature.
> 3. In some cases we have been able to provide some degree of external independent corroboration for the accuracy of their claims concerning what they are able to see in the physical world.
>
> Some of the cases are very compelling and overall the results are quite impressive.

HEAVEN IS WHAT YOU MAKE IT?

ARE near-death experiences about to prove survival of the self? Despite the problems the evidence is slowly tipping the scales in favour of the NDE researchers. If mind can exist without the physical body, does it automatically follow that there is a heaven?

Near-death experients and astral travellers describe some common characteristics, but their depictions of other worlds, although similar, are not identical. Herbert Philley, Petro Volpato and Ellen Robinson all described a 'bright beautiful land', but the fine details in all these and similar accounts tend to vary. For instance, Philley's 'heaven' was marred by disease-ridden people who populated ghettoes.

Heaven, *per se* might exist, but perhaps there is more than a grain of truth in the old saying; 'heaven is what you make it'. Maybe Herbert Philley has a strong social conscience.

Chapter 5

TIME AND AGAIN

A S WE have seen in Chapters 3 and 4 some people claim that they can astral travel to other dimensions. At the point of death a few of them even seem to go in an out-of-body state towards what may be an afterlife. Yet, if their claims are true, it is hard to imagine an eternity beyond death that stretches only one way.

If we live for ever *after* death, where was our eternal soul *before* we were born? Many religions across the world answer that perplexing question by asserting a belief in reincarnation. They say that we alternate our existence between periods of time spent in heaven and physical embodiment here on earth. In effect we live many lifetimes as different people.

This begs the question as to whether a study of apparent past life memories can help prove that we survive death. Indeed, can we learn more about the nature of an afterlife through knowledge of such incredible memories?

MEMORIES OF LONG AGO

WHAT is the first thing that you can remember? Perhaps a childhood home in which you are playing with a favourite toy. Memory tends to start around the age of two or three; anything earlier is considered unusual. So when they do occur, what do we make of these peculiar recollections? The following are fully conscious memories.

A middle-aged mother, June, reports how she sees herself alone in her room staring at the window as a dazzling light enters and floats around the Christmas tree. The light belongs to somewhere that she considers utterly beautiful and has all the colours of the rainbow inside. It exudes warmth and peace and she knows it to be a part of her 'real' home. Desperately she wants to return and feels like a prisoner trapped on earth. June was in her cot; this memory appears to come from the age of about three months.

Back to the womb

Clifford, a retired businessman, recalls being in a garden and feels very small as if surrounded by giants. He wants to stay here but feels unable to do so. Then silver spades start to dig at his body as if trying to pick him up. He feels light-headed and floating. Only later, when he learned the details of his birth, did these images start to be explained. He had been born by Caesarian section, and the silver spades could have been the scalpels used to 'dig him out'. It would appear as if Clifford was somehow conscious of his own birth.

According to science, recalling one's own birth is not possible

According to science, recalling one's own birth is not possible. Yet these stories of very early life recall are much more common with people who allege psychic experiences. We have collected evidence that those who claim to experience regular paranormal phenomena, such as NDEs, precognition and afterlife encounters, tend to have considerably better levels of memory from such an early age. Clearly something about the consciousness of such people facilitates this retention and makes them sense things which we describe as paranormal.

What of June's extraordinary memory? Is that light from a beautiful land with rainbow colours the place from which she came before being 'trapped on earth' by her birth? Is this 'real home' from which she has been exiled what we would term heaven?

Wise babies

Something else rather curious seems to be happening. Mike Oram from London puts it in this way: 'When I was very little – perhaps just a few months old – I remember thinking of the world as very strange indeed. It was full of people – adults – doing silly things. I understood them. I felt more sensible than they did. I was conscious of more than I should have been. It was as if I was an adult trapped in the body of a child. That is when I first realised that earth was not my real home.'

This sensation of being conscious in an adult, thinking way whilst still physically a baby is not uncommon. It is described in about 10 per cent of cases where people claim to have extraordinary degrees of early life recall.

Juliet, from a small Lancashire town, remembers an incident in her bedroom when she was only a few months old. Strange lights came to play with her. They appeared to open up her mind to a new awareness, as if childhood was an inconvenience and she could do far greater things than her body would allow. She developed abilities well ahead of her age, causing adults to refer to her as an 'old head on young shoulders'. It was as if inside she had already grown up, but her body would take many years to reach the same state.

According to our understanding of the development of the human mind, stories such as these can make no sense. These people ought to be young in mind as well as body. But what about their soul? Perhaps the essence of us all contains an eternal consciousness which can survive death. If so, can it also precede birth? Are we born with an inherent, well-developed consciousness that gets buried deep inside as our conscious experience throughout childhood swamps the rest of our life?

Nicola wanted her mother to explain why she was a girl when 'last time' she had been a boy

THE EYES OF A CHILD

WHEN Nicola Peart from Keighley in West Yorkshire was given a toy dog for her second birthday it sparked an extraordinary chain of events. She announced that it would be called Muff 'like the other dog I had'. But she had never owned a dog, real or otherwise.

Nicola, however, knew otherwise. She wanted her mother to explain why she was a girl when 'last time' she had been a boy, and stunned her family with an account of the time 'when Mrs Benson was my Mummy'. Much information was conveyed to them – her father was always dirty from working on the railway, they had lived in a stone house in Haworth, and the child had been killed on the railway line when struck by a steam engine. Indeed, so vivid was this last memory that when Nicola saw a TV image of a man falling off a railway bridge she screamed in terror.

Eventually the Pearts took her to Haworth – only a few miles away but a place that she had never visited before. They got lost, but Nicola led them straight to the old stone house about which she had spoken.

Investigations revealed that her fantastic story was true. The Bensons had indeed existed. The father had been a railwayman. Their son, born in 1875, had died as a small child – although the cause of death was not mentioned in the parish records. It seemed that Nicola might be remembering her past life one hundred years earlier, and doing so as if it were the most natural thing in the world.

Nicola is not alone. Children, often between the ages of about three and eight, come up with these spontaneous stories far more frequently than might be expected. Before she was two years old, Elspeth from Tyneside suddenly began to talk about her life as a nun, giving precise details of her clothing, convent, fellow nuns, day-to-day activities and the like. It scared her family.

By four she could remember the moment of her death and described it in awesome detail. She said that she had been praying when she suddenly collapsed and everything went dark. The next thing that she recalls is waking up in the company of nuns who had already died. They seemed to be welcoming her to heaven.

THE INVESTIGATORS

DR Ian Stevenson is a psychiatrist at the University of Virginia. His peers have said that he is either making an enormous error of judgement or will one day be ranked alongside Gallileo as one of the world's greatest scientists.

In 1957 Stevenson began to investigate stories about past lives from all over the world. His cases all stem from actual memories like those discussed so far in this chapter. Indeed he has said, 'The most promising evidence bearing on reincarnation seems to come from these spontaneous cases, especially among children.' In 1995, he told the journal *Reincarnation International* that evidence accrued by way of regression hypnosis – ie the taking back of a person in a hypnotic state in order to try to recall a past life memory – is not really acceptable on a scientific level.

Stevenson's focus on unsolicited conscious memories from children is important. However, there is a problem. In the majority of cases he has had to go to countries such as those on the Indian subcontinent where reincarnation is an accepted belief. Here children are not rebuked or

Some people believe Dr Ian Stevenson may be ranked alongside Galileo as one of the world's greatest scientists

dismissed as over-imaginative if they describe a past life. The downside is that they are indoctrinated into its alleged existence and complex rules virtually from birth, so fabrication becomes a lot more likely than in a country where this concept is not part of the culture. Indeed, it can be financially rewarding for one family to claim that their child is the reincarnation of a recently dead person of a higher and therefore richer caste.

An attempt at retribution?

At the age of two, Ravi Shankar told his parents of a previous life in which he had been murdered. Ravi has gone on to become one of India's most respected musicians

However, this last possible motive does not always apply. Ravi Shankar was born in Kanauj in the Uttar Pradesh region of India in 1951. But when he was two he announced that his father was actually called Jageshwar, describing this man's name, occupation and the place where he lived. This house was less than a mile away from the Shankars'.

The boy explained that in his other life he had been murdered by having his throat cut, and named the two people responsible. Then he pointed to his own throat, which bore a birthmark that resembled a knife wound.

Stevenson investigated this case some years later. The now teenage Ravi had no further memory of the affair – this is normal beyond the age of about seven or eight. Nonetheless the researcher spoke to many relatives who recalled the astonishing claims that had been made by the young boy. Nothing seems to have been gained by the Shankars through this episode – the Jageshwar family was no better off than they were. However, there was potentially a motive of a different kind at work.

As far as Stevenson could establish, Ravi's story was correct. A young boy had been murdered just as described some six months before Ravi was born, and the two suspects were those whom he had named. However, there was not enough evidence to lead to a conviction.

This provokes the speculation that the spirit of the murdered boy returned quickly to earth to try to express himself through Shankar and thus convict his own murderers. If so it did not work, because even in a country where reincarnation is readily accepted, a court would not convict an alleged murderer on this basis.

There is also a more rational possibility, if unprovable. The family of the murdered boy, incensed by the failure of the law could presumably have conspired with the Shankars. But Stevenson found no evidence to support a hoax and the birthmark remains to be taken into account.

Iowa memories

These child memories of other lives are being uncovered in great profusion now that we are alert to the possibility, and California psychotherapist Hemendra Banerjee has researched many of them. In one of his best cases, dating from 1980, three-year-old Romy Crees started to talk to her parents in Des Moines, Iowa, about her recent life as the thirty-seven-year-old father of three. The family were Catholics, a religion to which reincarnation is anathema, and were very upset.

But Romy insisted it was not a product of her imagination and poured out information about the life and death of a man named Joe Williams from Charles City, some 150 miles away. She could name Joe's wife and children, describe the house he was raised in, talk about his mother in endearing terms, and express terror at the motorcycle accident which had killed him.

Eventually Banerjee persuaded the Crees family to visit Charles City.

Romy responded as if she were going home, even insisting on buying a bunch of a particular kind of flowers for 'his' mother. They found the Williamses' house, even though it had been rebuilt after being struck by a tornado. A bewildered woman attempted to comprehend how a young girl from a city with which his family had no connection could possibly know so much intimate detail about her dead son.

Joe had been everything that Romy claimed. He did die in a motorcycle accident in 1975 – two years before Romy was born. The flowers selected were Mrs Williams' favourites. Romy knew things that could not have been read in newspaper reports of the accident, which had occurred far away in Chicago and made no national headlines. She even instantly picked Joe's photograph from among others in the house, seeming spontaneously to recognise 'himself'.

In situations such as these, what can we do but wonder if this is not proof of the continuance of the soul?

How could a small child from a strange city know so much intimate detail about Mrs Williams' dead son?

TOO CLOSE TO HOME?

*H*OWEVER, a nagging suspicion arises concerning the geographical proximity that is often involved. Stevenson's Indian cases concern reincarnation right on the doorstep: the children never recall lives in Katmandu or Birmingham. Two British girls were allegedly reborn later as twins to the same family. In the vast USA Romy Crees is only a short distance from the home of her supposed former life.

Why? Is it a cosmic law which brings souls back close to their former abode? A jump from country to country between the last life and the current one is fairly rare although there are plenty of examples where distances between lifetimes are not small. Joe Keeton, the hypnotherapist who has probably regressed more people than anyone else in Britain, says that his British subjects always recall previous lives in Britain. In our experiments with him that has certainly been the case.

Of course, motivation might well be a factor. If reincarnation is real and Joe Williams, for example, decided to return quickly to earth, then part of the plan might have been to relocate close enough to his former 'home' to allow this past life tracking process to occur. Perhaps it all led up to that meeting with 'his' mother in 1981 to prove to her that there is survival after death.

Indeed, it is notable that the shorter the gap between death in one life and rebirth into another, the shorter the distance between the two physical locations. This may suggest a plan at work. On the other hand,

Nicola Peart recalled a life just a couple of miles from her own birth-place and yet this had happened more than a century before. So the pattern is not a consistent one.

One possibility is that these children are simply 'tuning in' to information about the life of someone who once lived nearby. They could, in effect, be reading images from past events associated with an area. If these children are gifted at visual creativity (and some evidence suggests that they are), and if this extends into an enhanced capacity for psychic abilities, then perhaps they can somehow pick up the events from a life 'recorded' in the ether by some process we do not yet understand.

Yet, if so, why would these children all assume that these images are from their own past life, rather than correctly identify them as snapshots from the life of someone else? Also, why not detect the past life of a person living in the same house or neighbourhood? Although proximity is evident, it is rarely that close. Across the miles between past and present homes there must be thousands, perhaps millions, of possible lifetimes that would be open to this theoretical process of 'tuning in'. Why is one, and only one, selected from the many options?

The shorter the gap between death in one life and rebirth into another, the shorter the distance between the two physical locations

The spirits of the dead may seek out the minds of children because they are free from prejudice

Of course, another possibility is that the information is being conveyed from the afterlife by the surviving spirits of the dead people, who seek out and utilise the minds of children because they are free from prejudice and more open to psychic communications. These spirits may deliberately look for someone as near as possible to their home town, in the hope that their message would reach their loved ones and convince them of survival after death.

Again we must ask why there is no sign within these cases that the children reflected a message of survival sent from some heaven. The overwhelming drift seems to be that these children feel they were once the people whose lives they describe. Are they just making a mistake of origin, as some feel that mediums may do when they sense information and presume it comes from outside themselves?

UNDER THE INFLUENCE

THE popular assumption that the concept of reincarnation stands or falls through testimony imparted by means of hypnotic regression is shown to be groundless by the cases described in this chapter. Even if you dismiss every scrap of hypnotically produced evidence, a strong argument can still be made for the belief that our soul is eternal and alternates between sojourns in heaven and embodiment on earth.

Also bear in mind that the belief in reincarnation is remarkably widespread. It is not only a mainstay of religions with millions of followers such as Buddhism and Hinduism but it also dominated the cultures of societies as diverse as those of native Americans in Alaska and the ancient Chaldeans. Christianity is one major exception – and even there for several hundred years rebirth was accepted by the Christian Church. Indeed, certain phrases in the Bible can be interpreted as implying acceptance of reincarnation.

Nevertheless, many stories describing past life memories stem from hypnosis. What are we to make of these? During regression the mind engages in an exercise in imagination and reports the images that pop into it. There is no way to establish the origin of those images. They could be memory or they could just be fantasy. In experiments the information appears to be split about 50/50 between these two possibilities. The most probable source for past life memories conjured up under hypnosis is imagination harnessed to please the hypnotist. Even so, there could be true memories lurking in the subconscious similar to the childhood stories described earlier in this chapter. These could occasionally be freed through hypnosis to trigger 'genuine' cases. Just how does one tell which is which?

During regression the mind engages in an exercise in imagination and reports the images that pop into it

BARRIERS TO THE TRUTH

AN attempt to establish the veracity of past life evidence through historical records and similar checks is the only method that can help. Needless to say, there are problems. It is rare for the past life of any known historical character to be recalled – the vast majority are those of ordinary people. Highlights tend to be few, and are restricted to events common to all lives, such as births, marriages and deaths. This is precisely what you might expect if real memory were involved. Would not fantasy produce a far richer mixture of fame, fortune, glamour and action?

Unfortunately, routine lives are very hard to verify. Huge efforts are necessary to get the subject to give years, places, names and so on. This is true of memories of present lives too – feelings and emotions are more easily recalled than concrete details. Furthermore, parish records are incomplete until very recent times. Even if the regressed person is able to provide some of the required information, verification may still be impossible.

So most past lives are uncheckable. However, in the small percentage where research is possible does it prove the life to be real?

IN SEARCH OF YESTERDAY

THERE are quite a number of well-attested cases in which past life memories retrieved by hypnosis have been verified. The example of Reading man Ray Bryant, regressed by Joe Keeton to the life of soldier Reuben Stafford fighting in the Crimean War, is a good example. His military records were found in the barracks in Preston, miles from his home. Reuben's account of his death by drowning in London years after the war also matches the death certificate that was later uncovered. Some sceptics allege fraud – that Bryant somehow found these records and made up the past life. But this charge would seem to be untenable if

Reuben Stafford's death certificate below matched details remembered under hypnosis by Ray Bryant

CERTIFIED COPY OF AN ENTRY OF DEATH

Given at the GENERAL REGISTER OFFICE, LONDON.

Application Number 41864

No.	When and where died	Name and surname	Sex	Age	Occupation	Cause of death	Signature, description, and residence of informant	When registered	Signature of registrar
	REGISTRATION DISTRICT Poplar								
	1879. DEATH in the Sub-district of Poplar in the County of Mid								
Columns:—	1	2	3	4	5	6	7	8	9
97	Found dead Second April 1879 Millwall Dock	Reuben John Stafford	Male	52 yrs	Waterman	Violent Suffocation by drowning How caused not proved Millwall Dock	Certificate received from John Humphreys Coroner for Middlesex Inquest held Fourth April 1879	Tenth April 1879	Abraham Purdy Registrar

CERTIFIED to be a true copy of an entry in the certified copy of a Register of Deaths in the District above mentioned.

Given at the GENERAL REGISTER OFFICE, LONDON, under the Seal of the said Office, the 13th day of October 1983

DA 769509

This certificate is issued in pursuance of the Births and Deaths Registration Act 1953. Section 34 provides that any certified copy of an entry purporting to be sealed or stamped with the seal of the General Register Office shall be received as evidence of the birth or death to which it relates without any further or other proof of the entry, and no certified copy purporting to have been given in the said Office shall be of any force or effect unless it is sealed or stamped as aforesaid.

CAUTION:—Any person who (1) falsifies any of the particulars on this certificate, or (2) uses a falsified certificate as true, knowing it to be false, is liable to prosecution.

applied to the hundreds of similar cases worldwide. At least some of these witnesses cannot be deliberately fabricating. So where did these people get their information?

Can memory, like physical traits, be passed on genetically?

Genetic memory?

Many options have been suggested. A popular theory proposed by some radical scientists is that memory, like physical traits, may be passed on genetically. But a genetic link between a past and present life is exceptionally rare. Moreover, in numerous cases people died without children; the boy described by Nicola Peart, for instance, was clearly far too young to have passed on any genetic information before his death.

CRYPTOMNESIA

*T*HE one sceptical theory that does hold up is cryptomnesia. Scientific research has proved that the deeper levels of the mind retain memories of everything we have ever said and done. This area is shut off from normal conscious recall, but under hypnosis such data can flood out.

It is argued that past lives are built out of this store of images. Since the person describing the event can flesh out a skeleton of facts, for instance, an article read in the hairdresser's half a lifetime ago or a conversation overheard when a small child, then the past life takes on an air of credibility. They will deny quite honestly that they have ever heard a particular fact or name, but deep inside them lies some reference about which they have no conscious memory.

Cryptomnesia is a medical fact. Moreover, it has been proved to be the cause of one or two past life memories. For example, one woman who described her life as the wife of a Roman governor in Britain nearly two thousand years ago. Through luck and skill sceptic Melvyn Harris worked out that the story came from an obscure historical novel, which blended fact and fiction and included fictional characters, written fifty years earlier. Under hypnosis the woman must have tuned into dim memories of having read that book – an illustration of the awesome power of the mind.

For many this case establishes the truth about past life regression and quite possibly of reincarnation in general. If cryptomnesia was to blame here, why could it not explain every historically verifiable case? Since this is the simplest explanation, it is regarded by pragmatists as the truth.

However, it is not quite so simple. How could it explain the two very distinctive sources of information at different locations for the past life of Reuben Stafford? Surely Ray Bryant could not have stumbled across both sources by chance and then forgotten all about them? Cryptomnesia also has difficulty in accounting for the past life memories of very small children who would not have read historical novels and would have very limited access to other sources of cryptomnesia. And even in adults, without the special circumstances of hypnosis is it really likely to be at work?

Testing the evidence

We decided to conduct our own experiment with the help of psychoanalyst Dr Moyshe Kalman. The first few regressions produced nothing, but then an intriguing case was reported by Mark Simpson of the Northern Anomalies Research Organisation (NARO) and followed up with the help of investigator Alicia Leigh. It involved an elderly woman who had a bizarre memory that had first arisen many years ago and came to her spontaneously in the most unusual circumstances. Lillian first experienced her 'past life' in September 1951, when she was twenty-six and pregnant. Owing to complications she was rushed into hospital and hovered near death for three days. While she was in a coma she experienced a vision of a life from two hundred years before.

When her treachery in her past life as Mary was discovered, she was shot dead

'I was living in a place called Mells,' Lillian explained. 'My name was Mary. I was forty-five and lived in a big house as a cook.'

Lillian's vision also revealed that the house was near a factory that manufactured weapons and was owned by Mary's employer. An argument developed over the building of a new gun. Mary helped those workers opposed to it by stealing secret documents from her employer and hiding them in a wall near a canal. Her treachery was discovered and she was accidentally shot in the stomach, dying from her injuries.

'I know I didn't dream it,' Lillian said, recalling the vividness of the experience nearly half a century later. She had never heard of any place called Mells, but her family confirmed that after emerging from the coma she was a changed woman. It was almost as if she was adopting some of the lifestyle of her previous incarnation, including the way she did her hair.

Here are Lillian's own words, speaking on her deathbed as Mary, from a hypnosis session held on 9 November 1995 with Dr Kalman and Peter Hough. Questions have been removed, and some minor editing carried out, for the sake of clarity.

'In bed ... I feel so tired ... I went down the path towards the trees. There was a brick loose and I took it out. [I put in] a leather bag – with some paper inside. ... The master's papers.'

Mary says that her name is Turner, she gives the year as 1751 and offers family names for those whom she knows in the big house. Then she describes being shot by a mill worker. 'In the stomach... I don't feel so good now. I did it. It was my fault. I shouldn't have done it... I don't want to die now. ... There's a man stood in the corner. He's just stood watching me. I don't know who he is. I have never seen him before. He's dressed all in black. I was wondering why he was there when I was dying – when I died.'

Through Lillian, Mary then describes her own death. 'A long way to go. ... Let me go, please, let me go. ... I am on my own in the dark. It's a long way to come back... to hospital.'

At a further session more details emerged, including graphic descriptions of Mary Turner's early life in a very poor family. She claimed to have gone into service as a young child when her mother became ill and her brother was injured in the leg. Her other accounts of clothing, social life and minor details of the area were historically plausible. By now we knew that Mells was a real place, a small village in Somerset. Lillian had still never been there. Would her past life memories prove to have any validity?

Investigations into this case are still going on at the time of writing (mid-1996), but a few pointers have already emerged. Local historian Michael McGarvie states that there was a factory in the area which made tools but it was not, so far as is known, a gun-making factory. Near the River Mells was a large house, which was standing in 1751. The river was navigable, and boats passed along it carrying cotton. An old mill dating from the same era once stood close by – but it is unclear what it was used for at the appropriate time. More importantly, McGarvie tells us that there was a Turner family which leased some land from the Horners, a local landowning family, during the eighteenth century. But no contemporary parish records exist to establish if there was a Mary Turner who might have entered service in the big house and died in 1751. Records of deaths are also absent between 1749 and 1751.

At the conclusion of the hypnosis experiments it was decided to show Lillian a series of photographs. Of the nine pictures of villages and buildings, four had been taken in Mells and the other five in similar villages elsewhere. The only photograph that really struck a chord was one of the eighteenth century house, known in more recent times as the 'clothier's mansion', near the River Mells. Lillian said that this was very like the 'big house' in her vision, but added that the roof was not right. In fact it was a modern replacement.

'There's a man stood in the corner... He's dressed all in black'

ABOVE *The village of Mells, Somerset, today. To the right is the river and an old stone wall. Was this the wall where Mary hid the plans of a new gun?* RIGHT *St Andrew's Church was built in the fifteenth century yet Lillian, as Mary Turner, did not recognise it.* BELOW *The 'clothier's mansion' in Mells. Was this the 'big house' where Mary Turner died in 1751?*

*H*EAVEN IN MIND

*W*HAT does this experiment teach us about life after death? We were hoping that we might find subjects able to describe an afterlife in the same way that many offer vivid portraits of so-called past lives. Yet this was not the case. Here, Lillian's vision predated hypnosis and so this state clearly did not create her story. Certainly she was able to recall much more detail through regression – although whether this was memory or fantasy is impossible to say. Historical verification, whilst tantalising, remains difficult. Perhaps a novel set in Mells exists out there somewhere and triggered a complex form of cryptomnesia.

It is fascinating that the role-play and creativity of the hypnosis state so readily provoke 'past life' memories in nearly all attempts made to obtain them during experiments such as ours. Yet in all six attempts made before the arrival of Lillian, this same method failed to produce one coherent afterlife account.

This need not mean that there is no afterlife: such memories may simply not be accessible by this route. But the fact that subjects did not fantasise heavenly images may be important negative evidence.

When the first edition of this book was published in October 1996, Peter Hough sent Lillian a signed copy. About a week later he received a telephone call from her son, who had some sad news to convey.

After several months' illness, Lillian had passed away just a few days before Peter posted the book. Her son discovered the parcel on the doormat when he arrived at the house to sort through Lillian's belongings.

'It seemed too much of a coincidence, as if it was a sign,' he told Peter. 'When I read the title, *Life After Death and the World Beyond*, I felt someone was trying to tell me that my mother had survived death.'

Perhaps to return again?

Chapter 6

TV HEAVEN

IN OUR book *The Afterlife* we reported on electronic voice phenomena or EVP – anomalous voices captured on audiotape and purportedly belonging to the dead. As we were finishing that book, an even more amazing phenomenon was overtaking it: television pictures, computer images and faxes of the deceased transmitted from the 'other side'.

On the face of it, this is one of the most exciting developments in survival research – exciting because it is so accessible. Here we have 'evidence' that anyone can see and hear: recorded voices, printed out messages and pictures of heaven captured on videotape transmitted by deceased scientists! But how did it all begin?

ELECTRONIC VOICE PHENOMENA

DURING the nineteenth century Thomas Edison tried to perfect a machine which could communicate with spirits, but failed. In 1959 Swedish film producer Friedrich Jurgenson captured voices on tape whilst recording birdsong. This was in a remote part of the countryside, and the voices were actually discussing the bird sounds. Jurgenson experimented and picked up the voices of deceased friends and relatives who apparently spoke to him. The results were published in a remarkable book entitled *Voices from the Universe*.

This encouraged scientists such as Professor Hans Bender, director of the state-run parapsychological laboratory at the University of Freiburg

While recording birdsong in a remote part of the countryside, Friedrich Jurgenson captured unexplained voices on tape

During the nineteenth century Thomas Edison (pictured right in his laboratory) tried, without success, to pioneer a machine which could communicate with spirits

in Germany, and Dr Konstantin Raudive, based in Latvia, to carry out their own experiments. Physicist Dr Alex Schneider and engineering specialist Theodor Rudolph joined the team, and together they recorded around one hundred thousand anomalous short phrases. However, critics such as Cambridge student David Ellis, who carried out a two-year study, concluded that some of the voices probably came from stray Russian radio broadcasts, while others were difficult to hear and owed more to the imagination than to discarnate entities.

In subsequent experiments in the early 1970s equipment was fully screened to stop stray radio signals intruding on the tape, with amazing results. Engineers from the electronics firm Pye began the experiment with an attitude of scepticism, but by the end of the session were convinced that something very odd was happening. Hundreds of anomalous words and phrases were recorded. Leading researchers Sarah Estep, president of the American EVP Association, as well as Raymond Cass and Gilbert Bonner in Britain have produced some intriguing results – recorded voices that seem to be attempting to contact researchers on this side of the veil.

SPIRICOM

REMARKABLE though some people thought they were, in essence the experiments only produced anomalous words or phrases. Often the names of researchers were heard. Critics, however, have pointed out that often one heard what one wanted to hear. This ambiguity was to change in 1977 when wealthy American inventor George Meek claimed he had built a machine that allowed two-way conversations with the dead.

Meek was in regular contact with two entities, 'Doc Nick' and 'Dr Mueller'. The latter provided intimate details of his life on earth which could mostly be corroborated, and even advised on how the equipment could be improved. Meek said he would freely pass on the designs so that others could duplicate his results.

Naturally Spiricom – short for 'spirit communications' – came in for a lot of controversy, and some critics asserted it was an obvious hoax. The main operator of the equipment was an electronics technician called Bill O'Neil. Certainly when O'Neil was not about nothing much seemed to happen, but it was thought that O'Neil was acting as a medium for the entities and not involved in a fraud. Neither Meek nor O'Neil seemed to want to make any money from the project.

Mueller spoke in a strange synthesised voice that some likened to the sound produced by an artificial larynx, but sceptics could not reproduce the effect. Eventually Dr Mueller moved on to a higher plane, but not before predicting that the next step would be communication through television. Was this a further development in an elaborate hoax, or a prediction that eventually bore fruit?

In April 1982 George Meek held a press conference in Washington to pass on details of the equipment used in the Spiricom project. After Meek's presentation the questions put by TV, radio and newspaper

American inventor George Meek claimed to have built a machine that allowed two-way conversations with the dead

journalists reflected a genuine interest in his work. However, the newspaper headlines told a more whimsical story after editors and sub-editors had put a different spin on it. Nevertheless researchers in Europe were determined to build on Meek's success.

THE DEAD – LIVE ON AIR

ONE of those who picked up the gauntlet was a German electronics engineer called Hans Otto Koenig. Nine months after Meek's press conference, Koenig was invited by Radio Luxembourg to demonstrate his new ultrasound device, which he claimed could duplicate O'Neil's conversations with the dead.

'Koenig's Generator' was connected to the station's broadcasting system under the supervision of station engineers and switched on. No one knew what, if anything, to expect.

Once the device was operational, one of the engineers asked Koenig if voices would come through on request. Within seconds an unexpected voice replied: 'Otto Koenig makes wireless with the dead.' Everyone in the studio was astounded; the programme's presenter, Rainer Holbe, affirmed to his audience that no trickery was involved. Another question was asked, and a reply came through the speakers: 'We hear your voice.' Staff and engineers were convinced that the source of the voices was paranormal.

Within seconds an unexpected voice replied: 'Otto Koenig makes wireless with the dead'

Meek flew over to Germany and attended a demonstration of the equipment in Koenig's laboratory. He was accompanied by a colleague, a distinguished scientist called Dr Ralf Determeyer. The equipment was minutely examined for fraud, and then the demonstration began. Meek was astounded: Koenig had managed to duplicate his own success. One voice after another came through in conversation with those present. Voice pattern analysis between Koenig's paranormal induced voices, and recordings made when the personalities were alive, proved to be almost identical.

Vidicom

The leap from audio to video came a year later, in 1985. A Swiss electronics expert called Klaus Schreiber had been studying Meek's designs, and from them developed what he called 'Vidicom'. This consisted of an adapted television set which was not attached to an aerial. The machine was switched on with a video camera pointed at the screen to record any images. Over the next four years, until his death, Schreiber picked up many photographic images of people whom he recognised as deceased relatives and friends.

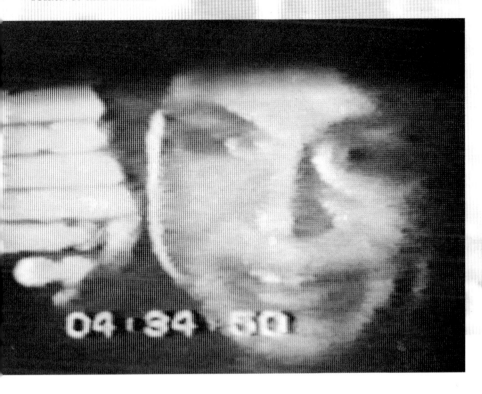

INSTRUMENTAL TRANSCOMMUNICATION?

'EVP' failed to describe this new development accurately, so a new term was coined – instrumental transcommunication, or ITC for short. Was the spirit world really following earthly technological development from wireless to television? Certainly it fired the imaginations of afterlife believers and researchers, but were the amazing pictures the result of inter-dimensional communication or blatant fraud?

The man who started off EVP research, Friedrich Jurgenson, died in 1987. On the day of his funeral a former colleague, Claude Thorlin, recorded an image of Jurgenson on his television set. Since then, several deceased EVP researchers have turned up on television screens. An image of Dr Mueller appeared on equipment belonging to a German ITC group headed by Adolph Homes. Was Mueller fulfilling his prediction, or was this just another link in a chain of deception?

The above image was captured on TV screen by the Harsch-Fishbachs in 1988. It was recognised as one Hanna Buschbeck, president of the German EVP Association before her death aged seventy-four. Here she looks in her late twenties. Note the strange configuration of the hand, with six rather odd-looking digits

TIMESTREAM

MAGGY Harsch-Fishbach from Luxembourg began experimenting with EVP in 1984. Initially her husband, Jules, was sceptical, but some positive results later convinced him of the paranormal origins of the voices. The couple were contacted by spirits on a link dubbed the 'Eurosignal Bridge'. In 1986 a voice advised them to disconnect their television aerial and switch on the set to an untuned channel. The Harsch-Fishbachs did as they were told and set up a video camera.

Jules and Maggy Harsch-Fishbach claim to have developed two-way communication with the spirit world using television sets, computers, telephones and fax machines

The couple noticed several images flash across the screen – too quickly for any detail to be discerned. They recorded for about ten minutes, then replayed the tape at a much reduced speed. Within a few frames the image of a man appeared – a deceased relative, the main communicator through the Eurosignal Bridge. During a subsequent message he informed the Harsh-Fishbachs that a research team was being organised on the Other Side, and that they were to do the same on earth.

The couple duly founded the Cercle d'Etudes sur la Transcommunication (CETL) which translates as the Study Circle in Transcommunications. Shortly afterwards a being calling himself 'Technician' made contact, informing them that it was his job to coordinate research and communications between the two parties. Technician informed them when a message or image was about to be transmitted, so that they could record it.

The Harsch-Fishbachs and their team developed two-way communication with the entity. In 1988 he informed them that they had been selected by the spirit communicators, who called the project 'Timestream', to help them improve the link between the two worlds. After this the communications expanded to include computers, telephones and fax machines.

Personalities from the past

The Timestream participants consisted of a host of famous personalities, including the nineteenth-century British explorer Sir Richard Burton,

Friedrich Jurgenson, Konstantin Raudive and Thomas Edison. In April 1995 the Harsch-Fishbachs received a fax purportedly from science fiction author Jules Verne, who died in 1905. Apparently the style conforms to that of the French writer. With it was a picture of a clean-shaven Verne wearing a modern high-necked tunic.

The Timestream operators were also in touch with other ITC groups, although CETL were the main contactees. Without doubt the central attraction of the alleged communications are the pictures supposedly showing the Timestream operators at work. Ironically, these are also its main weakness.

The Timestream participants included the explorer Sir Richard Burton and the inventor Thomas Edison

Every picture tells a story

After a while a female spirit communicator named Swejen Salter took over the job of Technician, forming a close bond with the Harsch-Fishbachs. On 28 April 1992 an image of Friedrich Jurgenson appeared on a television screen in Germany belonging to Adolph Homes. According to CETL, an image of Swejen Salter simultaneously materialised on their computer, standing alongside a screen showing the identical picture of Juergenson. The problem with the image of Swejen Salter is that it looked very like Maggy Harsch-Fishbach!

In 1991 CETL produced a picture which it claimed had been received paranormally. It appeared to show film director George Cukor and Thomas Edison in the Timestream sending station – a place equipped just like a contemporary earthly laboratory. Even more amazingly, Edison, who died in 1931, was wearing the style of suit, shirt and tie worn in the 1990s! Intriguingly, there is a strong resemblance between the modern Edison and his image photographed just before his death. This cropped up again on another CETL-produced picture, involving a close friend of the Harsch-Fishbachs.

Ernst Mackes died on 26 November 1992 after a long illness. On 4 February 1993 the Harsch-Fishbachs claim to have received a letter from him on their computer. In it he gave a vivid description of the paradise that he now inhabited, which he referred to as 'Marduk':

Edison was wearing the fashions of the 1990s even though he had died sixty years earlier

> At the moment I am sitting here under a roof of exotic palm tree leaves. Above me is the light of our three suns. Temperatures are very moderate, and in the clear morning air numerous multi-coloured hummingbirds are buzzing around me.
>
> Butterflies of incredible beauty, some of them as large as soup plates, are flapping their wings and settle down on blossoms and

plants. Before me is a refreshing glass of lemonade. In the distance, the sunlight is reflecting in the river of eternity, which is visible behind a yellow sand beach.

A month later a picture of Ernst appeared on the Harsch-Fishbachs' computer. It showed him seated at a computer against a backdrop of palm trees, and was supposedly sent by Swejen Salter.

Two pictures which some people consider to be of a very dubious nature were produced by Klaus Schreiber and Adolph Homes. Schreiber produced an image of a dead Austrian abbot called Dr Wiesinger. Comparison with an old photograph of the abbot shows them to be identical. The background and the clothing are different but otherwise they are exact, even down to the shadows falling across the right-hand side of the face. The same can be stated of a picture said to have been paranormally produced on television by Adolph Homes. It shows George Meek's Dr Mueller. When viewed next to a photograph of Mueller, who died in 1967, it can be seen that it is remarkably similar, including the way the shadows fall on the face.

PICTURES FROM HEAVEN?

ARE images of the dead really materialising on computer and television screens, or is this just a modern manifestation of the hoaxed spirit photographs from Victorian times? At the turn of the century, enterprising photographers were producing 'spirit' faces of the deceased which appeared around the heads of living relatives in studio pictures. Some of these modern spirit images seem as dubious as their Victorian counterparts. Writer and researcher Roy Stemman commented in *Psychic News* that 'it is curious, if those in the Beyond are trying to produce a scientific and psychic breakthrough, that they have to rely on old and doctored library photos'.

The easy and straightforward answer is that they are fraudulently produced. However, if that is so it involves a conspiracy between several groups of people, and this would not be easy to maintain. Could it be that the ITC researchers are the victims of hoaxers? Could hackers have found a way into their computer systems? Or could the pictures be frauds produced paranormally by mischievous entities?

Sceptics will scoff at the idea of computer workshops and idyllic locations existing on the 'other side' in what is supposedly a non-physical

Are the spirit pictures being seen on computer and television screens a modern manifestation of the hoaxed spirit photographs from Victorian times? This nineteenth century photograph is captioned 'Mr and Mrs Lacey and a visitor from Beyond'

dimension. CETL have an explanation, derived, they say, from the spirit entities themselves via telephone calls and computer messages.

The spirit entities have bodies composed of an etheric substance of a higher vibration than their earthly hosts. There are no diseases, and everyone ages up or down to resemble a physical age of between twenty-five and thirty. They live in furnished homes amid beautiful landscapes on 'the third astral level' – a 'planet' called Marduk. Sex is still possible, and the beings eat food which is materialised by thought. Although there is no physical pain, mental anguish still exists.

In CETL's image of heaven everyone ages up or down to look somewhere between twenty-five and thirty

CETL's US spokesman and president of Continuing Life Research, Mark Macey, explained that in his view the spirit worlds are created by the power of thought. The form of the creation is derived from the memories and expectations of former earth-bound beings. 'They manifest astral bodies that look like the familiar physical bodies they left behind. They manifest clothes not because they need clothes but because they had grown accustomed to wearing them on earth.'

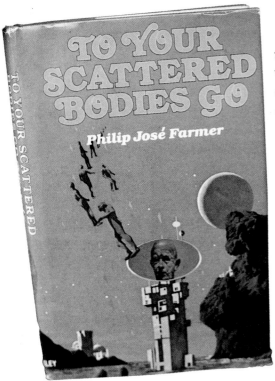

The first of a series of novels which told the story of the dead resurrected on the bank of a huge river. There, explorer Richard Burton searches for answers to the enigma. This predated the claims by ITC researchers

RIVERWORLD

ACCORDING to CETL researchers, a feature of the world known as Marduk is a single large waterway called the River of Eternity. One of the alleged spirit communicators, as previously mentioned, is that of the explorer Sir Richard Burton. According to CETL he has told them of his journeys through the astral planes and his adventures along the River of Eternity.

This sounds like a good plot for a novel – as indeed it was in 1971. That year saw publication of *To Your Scattered Bodies Go*, the first in the highly acclaimed Riverworld series written by Philip José Farmer. The main character in that series is Burton, who after dying at the hands of an Arab finds himself resurrected on the banks of an enormous river. The explorer is not alone. He finds the company of other people, famous in their day, and begins his exploration of the Riverworld.

Furthermore, ancient astronaut researcher Zecharia Sitchin claims that life on earth was seeded by human-like beings from a planet that returns to our stellar vicinity every few thousand years. He published early work on the subject in a book called *The Twelfth Planet* back in 1978. Sitchin names the mystery planet as Marduk.

DOUBTS AND PROBLEMS

WHAT are we to make of this – a coincidence beyond the bounds of coincidence? Do these links prove the reality, or the fallacy, of CETL's claims? Or are the CETL researchers victims themselves of hoaxers tapping into their equipment and leaving significant clues about the origin of their handiwork?

ITC research has the potential to produce scientific proof of the existence of life beyond physical death, and its continuance in a place which we might call the 'other side', 'paradise' or 'heaven'. To their credit the CETL researchers have not sought to make money from their material and have shunned publicity. Jules and Maggy Harsch-Fishbach still work full-time as teachers. However, much of the work is so riddled with suspicion that it casts doubt on its overall credibility.

In September 1995 ITC researchers from around the world met at a secret location in Cornwall to discuss the future of research. As a result an organisation was set up to foster better communications between experimenters. It was called INIT – International Network for Instrumental Transcommunication.

When Peter Hough wrote to Mark Macey asking him to clarify answers to some of the problems associated with the contacts, the American replied that he would only correspond if he was convinced Hough would give ITC researchers a fair hearing. Peter wrote back detailing previous books where contentious material had been treated objectively. Macey did not reply. If the deceased really are communicating using modern technology, then this attitude is unhelpful. Without an unprejudiced exchange of information we will be no nearer learning the truth about the possibility of an afterlife.

Chapter 7

MESSENGERS FROM BEYOND

TIED in with the concept of heaven in many religions is a belief in angels. However, for a long time now angels, like fairies, have been regarded as the province of children or peasants – the idea that they should be taken seriously is treated with derision, or at best embarrassment, by sophisticated adults. Yet, curiously, as we approach the end of the twentieth century, there has been a rise in the number of reports of encounters with angels, and the belief in guardian angels is particularly strong.

Why this increase in angel contacts? Are more incidents occurring, or is it just that more are being reported? With a growing interest in all things 'supernatural', perhaps the climate is currently kinder and more patient with those brave enough to make such events public? Are visitors from heaven objectively real beings? If not, does this cast doubt on the reality of heaven too?

> *To sceptics, the increase in reports of angels may indicate nothing more than a passing fad*

OPPOSITE PAGE *A detail from the painting of the Annunciation by Fra Angelico (c 1387-1455) showing the Angel Gabriel*

Sceptics might argue that the increase in reports and books on the subject, from both sides of the Atlantic, is merely indicative of a new fad and signifies nothing more. However, a counter-argument would be that

the more people talk openly about something potentially embarrassing, the more other people are inclined to follow suit.

Natalie Rimmer came forward with her story after hearing Peter Hough give a radio broadcast. She presented her account in a highly articulate and convincing manner.

SEEING AN ANGEL

IN August 1993 Natalie and Jeremy Rimmer had been married for only a year when Jeremy's mother died at home suddenly while they were on holiday. Grief-stricken, Jeremy started having a recurring dream. In it he would meet his mother and ask her why she had died, and what was it like to be dead. Her reply was: 'I can't answer you that.' Then one evening a remarkable thing happened which involved Natalie.

In the early hours, Natalie suddenly awoke to find the room bathed in a brilliant white light

---

The couple went to bed as usual. In the early hours, Natalie suddenly awoke to find the room bathed in a brilliant white light. 'I was wide awake but I lay still, my eyes drawn towards the strongest point of light which came through our bedroom door.'

As Natalie struggled to rationalise the phenomenon an overwhelming feeling of peace, love and harmony washed over her. She turned her head to look at her still sleeping husband and saw the outline of a woman sitting on his side of the bed. 'To say I saw an outline is not entirely accurate. She had no real form as such, except for a clear head shape. Her body was swathed in a white cloak which blended into the light. She appeared young – in her early or middle twenties perhaps – and her fair hair, which merged into the light, was tied back in a black band.'

Natalie watched as the being leaned across Jeremy and lovingly stroked his head. Three times she performed this action before she became aware of Natalie observing her. The woman was absorbed slowly into the light; then it too left. For a while Natalie wondered whether she should wake her husband and tell him of the incident; then Jeremy woke up of his own accord.

They discussed the visit and wondered whether the figure was the spirit of Jeremy's mother as a young woman, or an angel sent to comfort him. Natalie feels that she was allowed to witness the event to aid her healing, and that it was a sign that her mother-in-law was safe and well. She was at pains to impress on us the reality of the experience. 'All through the experience I enjoyed the beautiful peaceful feeling, and at no time did I feel afraid or wary of the stranger at the side of our bed. I was absolutely wide awake; this was a real experience and not a dream.'

I was absolutely wide awake; this was a real experience and not a dream'

HEARING AN ANGEL

IF guardian angels do exist, can they save a person from certain death? Travel guide Shari Peterson was used to flying and had no particular interest in angels until 24 February 1985. On that date she left Denver, Colorado, on Flight 811 bound for Auckland, New Zealand.

'Tighten your seat belt,' said a sudden disembodied voice. 'You're in for the ride of your life!'

The Boeing 747 refuelled in Honolulu, then took off again and climbed to cruising altitude. Shari had been upgraded from the back of the aircraft to row thirteen. She loosened her safety belt, reclined the seat and became engrossed in a novel. Suddenly her attention was interrupted by a loud voice which said clearly: 'Tighten your seat belt. You're in for the ride of your life!'

Shari twisted round but there was no one there. She tried to get back into the book but could not concentrate. 'That's not what one person would say to another,' she thought, and decided she had nothing to lose by doing as the voice said and refastening her belt. Sixty seconds later the side of the aircraft peeled away like a tin of sardines. Rows eight to twelve were gone and Shari Peterson saw passengers around her being sucked out through the 15 by 20 foot hole in the fuselage. There is no doubt that if she had not fastened her seat belt she too would have died.

Miraculously the aircraft managed to return and land safely at Honolulu. But while it was losing altitude another passenger heard a voice too. A husband who was clinging on to his wife to stop them both

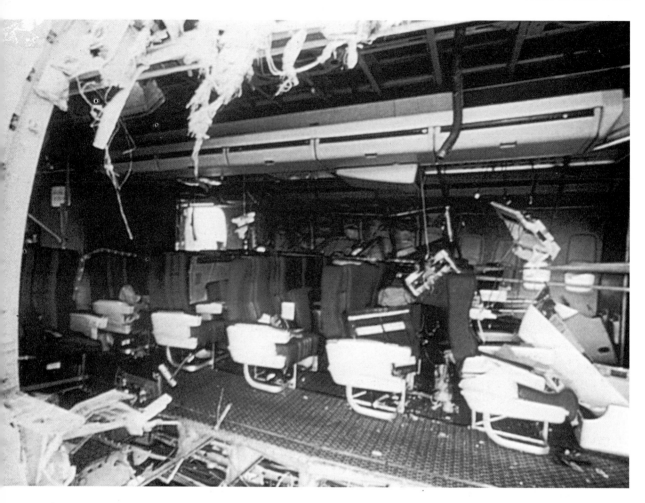

The wreckage of the Boeing 747 on which Shari Peterson was travelling. Shari believes her guardian angel saved her from almost certain death

being sucked out heard a voice say: 'Sir, it's not your time. Relax, it's going to be okay. You're going to be all right.'

They were, as was Shari Peterson. When the United States Navy recovered the cargo door from the sea bed they discovered that a short circuit had opened it in flight. There had been no warning, no possible indication that something was about to go wrong.

MEETING A LIVING ANGEL

THE British chemist Sir Humphry Davy, who died in 1829, had a chain of experiences with an 'angel' which he could never satisfactorily explain. Later he wrote a report of these events.

He first related how he caught typhus while working in a prison. 'My illness was severe and dangerous; as long as the fever continued, my dreams or deliriums were painful and oppressive; but when the weakness and exhaustion came on, and when the probability of death seemed to my physicians greater than that of life, there was an entire change.'

Davy described his state as 'senseless', but strangely his mind was 'peculiarly active'. In this condition he was visited by the form of a beautiful young woman. The visits occurred over a number of days, during which Davy 'engaged in the most interesting and intellectual conversation'. He noted: 'Her figure for many days was so distinct in my mind as to form almost a visual image: as I gained strength the visits of my good angel, for so I called it, became less frequent, and when I was restored to health they were altogether discontinued.'

He described her as having brown hair, blue eyes and bright rosy cheeks. Davy was at pains to point out that in no way was she a reflection of his sexual fantasies – indeed, at the time he was madly in love with a woman who had black hair, dark eyes and a pale complexion.

Two twists to the story came ten and twenty years later, when he came across the living image of the angel who had visited his bedside. He first met her during his travels in Illyria, now part of former Yugoslavia, when she was a girl of fourteen or fifteen. Ten years after that he developed a serious illness and was nursed back to health by the same young woman whom he had met previously.

The great scientist tried to rationalise the affair, but could not. If the angel was just a product of his delirium, surely she should have taken on the appearance of his internal fantasies, or at least resembled someone he knew. That he should then meet her physical counterpart, who ten years afterwards nursed him back to health, poses a series of events too awesome to trivialise as 'coincidence'.

On two later occasions he came across the living image of the angel who had visited his bedside

THE PATIENCE OF ANGELS

ANGELS, it seems, can be our psychological and physical salvation. Dr Melvin Morse has catalogued many such cases but was surprised to learn that Dr Frank Oski, his former tutor at Johns Hopkins University in Baltimore, had his own story to tell.

Burdens will pass

Dr Oski is a professor of paediatrics. As a student he became frustrated by the limitations of medicine when it came to saving children dying of congenital defects. One night he went to bed perturbed by the fact that

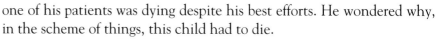

one of his patients was dying despite his best efforts. He wondered why, in the scheme of things, this child had to die.

About an hour after falling asleep he was awoken by a bright, intense ball of light which had invaded the room. In the light he could make out the form of a woman. She looked about twenty, and had wings on her back. Dr Oski lay there in shock while she explained why some children had to die.

In a quiet, reassuring voice she told him that life was not a single event but a continuous cycle during which both physical and spiritual defects were improved. Most people had this knowledge revealed to them when they died. Handicapped people were aware of this intuitively, enduring their problems with remarkable restraint because they 'knew' that their burdens would pass. Some children were endowed with the purpose of using their affliction to teach the rest of us how to love.

Dr Oski was brave enough to talk publicly of his experience, requesting that his peers keep an open mind.

The woman in white

Morse heard the following story from a nurse. A ten-year-old boy suffering 80 per cent burns died in hospital of an infection, and on the two previous nights the nurse had observed a strange phenomenon: a woman in white standing at the boy's bedside. The first time she thought it was an unauthorised visitor, and prepared to challenge her. But as the nurse approached, the figure disappeared. The following night the woman appeared again. For a while the nurse observed her apparently talking to the boy. Once again the woman vanished when she attempted to approach.

When the boy's condition started to deteriorate the hospital staff fought hard to save him, but in vain. Afterwards the saddened nurse went into a utility room to cry for half an hour. When she came out and headed towards her ward, she saw the lady in white ahead of her. The figure was walking down the corridor – hand in hand with the little boy.

AN ANGEL TO THE RESCUE

CAN 'guardian angels' intercede to prevent a crime? One of Melvin Morse's most remarkable cases was told to him by the wife of a well-known television presenter.

She was driving on a busy main road when her car developed a problem, so after pulling on to a quieter road she sat and waited for the police to arrive. A car pulled up in front of her, and when the driver came over to her she foolishly wound down the window. He reached inside, snatched the keys from the ignition, ordered her to move over and got in beside her. Then, after pulling out a gun, he ordered her to take off her clothes. The terrified woman was certain that she was about to be raped or shot.

Suddenly the car was filled with an intense bright light. The woman looked behind her, hoping that another car had arrived, but the road was dark and empty. Then she realised that the light was actually inside the vehicle – right between them. In the light appeared the form of a man. She felt an instant rapport with this being, but it was too much for the would-be attacker who got out, ran back to his own car and drove off at speed. When she was safe again the figure vanished.

The woman told Dr Morse that she believed her guardian angel had appeared that night, and saved her from certain rape and possible murder.

Do supernatural presences bring help and comfort to human beings in distress and danger? Are angels more than imagination and wish fulfilment? Can science prove that experients 'see' objectively existing entities? Scientific research into visions of another messenger from heaven – the Virgin Mary – strongly indicate that proof is on its way.

Chapter 8

VISITS BY THE VIRGIN

VISIONS of the Virgin Mary have been reported for centuries by Catholics in many countries, particularly in simple rural communities. Does this mean that the mother of Jesus returns to earth and imparts messages from heaven? Or is it just a psychological response on the part of willing believers? Intriguingly, over the last few years scientific evidence has been produced to demonstrate that these are genuine encounters with *something*.

THE CULT OF MARY

THE familiar Bible story tells us that Mary, betrothed to a carpenter called Joseph, was visited by the angel Gabriel. At this time she was still a virgin. Gabriel told her she had 'found favour with God' and would conceive a son, whom she was to call Jesus. Joseph not unnaturally thought she had been unfaithful and decided to dissolve the relationship quietly. While he was considering this, an angel appeared to him in a dream and said that Mary was in fact filled with the 'Holy Spirit'. The birth had been prophesied with the words: 'Behold, a virgin shall conceive and bear a son. ...'

This episode is recounted in only two of the four Gospels, those of Matthew and Luke. Indeed, Mary is something of a bit-part player in the New Testament, and after her fifteen minutes of fame sinks quietly into the background. Why then was her status enhanced by the Catholic Church almost to the point of deification? Was it to counter the popularity of paganism, and its deity the Earth Mother?

In place of the Earth Mother

There are indications that the Earth Mother was worshipped in England at least as far back as AD 98. The Great Goddess was venerated under a variety of guises in different parts of the world two thousand years before Christ. Early Christians found that the goddess, who combined the attributes of Earth Mother and lover, was very popular and could not be banished. People preferred this soft matriarchal symbol to the overtly patriarchal image of Christianity.

Some commentators believe that it was for this reason that at the Council of Ephesus in AD 431 Mary, mother of Jesus, was elevated to become the Virgin Mary, Mother of God. Popular historical writer Geoffrey Ashe argues that without this hyperdulia or super-veneration of Mary the new religion Christianity would have died. It was a masterful move that supplanted the Earth Mother with Mary and made the conversion of pagans to Christianity so much easier.

Wherever Catholicism spread, so did veneration of the Virgin Mary; across Europe and South America she became the prime focus for adoration. The cult really took off in the seventeenth century when writers such as Grignon de Montford actively encouraged the faithful to direct their attentions away from God and towards Mary. They claimed inside knowledge that God wished to be worshipped through her.

A WISH IS GRANTED

CAN religious indoctrination cause believers to hallucinate, or does a positive state of mind create the conditions in which entities can manifest? French nun Catherine Laboure wished fervently to see the 'Blessed Virgin'. On 17 July 1830 she and her fellow sisters had been instructed on devotion to the saints and in particular the mother of Jesus. The following evening she went to bed believing that a meeting would actually take place. Catherine recorded in her diary what happened:

> I was sleeping when at 11.30 I heard my name: 'Sister, Sister, Sister Catherine!' I lifted my curtain and saw a child of about five or six, dressed completely in white, who said, 'Come with me to the chapel: the Blessed Virgin is waiting for you!' I dressed quickly and followed the child. He went on my left, and from him came rays of light. To my great astonishment there were lights shining brightly all along our way. My amazement was at its height when I saw the candles and torches of the chapel lit as if for a midnight mass.

'Come with me to the chapel: the Blessed Virgin is waiting for you!'

A moment later, the child said, 'Here is the Blessed Virgin!' I heard the rustling of a silken robe coming from the side of the sanctuary. The Lady bowed to the tabernacle, then sat down in the chaplain's chair.

Despite all this, Catherine was uncertain whether the figure really was Mary. Sensing her doubts, the 'child' tried to reinforce them. His voice deepened into a man's and he repeated that this was indeed the Virgin. Belief flooded through the girl and she rushed forward and knelt before the figure. 'I am certain this was the happiest moment of my life,' she wrote.

The Blessed Virgin spoke to me about my conduct towards my director, and confided some things which I may not reveal. I don't know how much time passed. When she left it was like a light going out; she disappeared like a shadow, as she had come. 'She has gone,' said the child. Together we went back. When I returned to the dormitory it was two o'clock in the morning.

The passing on of 'secrets' is a general feature of encounters with paranormal entities. UFO abductees often claim that the being they meet have told them things about the future of the earth and their own lives which they must not divulge.

BERNADETTE AT LOURDES

THE shrine at Lourdes in south-western France is world-famous for its 'miracle' healing. Every year thousands of pilgrims flock there praying to Mary and hoping for a cure. It all started more than a hundred years ago with a fourteen-year-old girl called Bernadette Soubirous.

The crowd were aghast when Bernadette put soil into her mouth and vomited

---

On 11 February 1858 Bernadette began having visions of the Virgin, which continued until July. Over this period huge crowds gathered. On 25 February some three hundred watched in amazement as Bernadette began clawing at the earth: she had been instructed to dig by the vision. The crowd were aghast as she put soil into her mouth and vomited. Then, where she had been digging, a spring emerged in which she washed. It produced 18 gallons of water a day and became the central focus of the shrine that was subsequently built there.

The statue of the Apparition in the Grotto at Lourdes, France, marking the spot where Bernadette Soubirous had visions of the Virgin Mary in 1858

Official miracles?

There are many stories of remarkable cures at Lourdes, but only a small minority survive the arduous formal investigation by Church officials. This is required before a healing is accepted as miraculous. In spite of the thousands of pilgrims who flock to the shrine every year, only a mere sixty-five cures have been accepted as 'official' miracles. Currently, two cases are being considered by the Lourdes Medical Bureau.

Kazik Stepan was seventeen when he was struck down with brain cancer, and deemed incurable by specialists at Guy's Hospital, in London. The cure came about when his bishop offered mass for him at Lourdes. At that instant, back home in Britain, nurses were amazed to see the dying youth suddenly sit up and smile. He subsequently made a full recovery, married and had children, and now, aged forty-seven, is a headmaster in Warsaw, Poland.

Jacques Salaun had suffered multiple sclerosis for seventeen years when he was taken to Lourdes. Almost totally paralysed, he was confined to a wheelchair and knew that death was not far away.

While staying in the Sainte Bernadette Hospital, Jacques saw a vision of the Virgin Mary. The figure, wearing a white robe, ordered him to stand up. Jacques was unable to carry out the order, but left Lourdes comforted.

Back home at Chartrès something took control of his body. Jacques experienced intense cold followed by an unbearable burning sensation. Minutes later his claw-like hands unclenched, and he was able to rise from his wheelchair and walk across the room. Doctors can now find no trace of the disease.

FURTHER VISITS BY THE VIRGIN

VALLENSANGES, a small village near St Etienne in central France, became the location for a visit by the Virgin Mary in 1888. The inhabitants were poor, pious peasants. None was more devoted than thirteen-year-old Jean Bernard, the eldest of five children. Rather than play with other boys, Jean preferred to visit a crude chapel he had built which contained a statuette of the Virgin.

On the morning of 19 July Jean's mother sent him out to collect firewood. While doing so he saw a lizard and looked around for a stone with which to kill it. When he turned back to the creature he was astounded to see a foot resting on it.

The foot belonged to a *grande dame*, who was extremely beautiful. She was wearing a white dress, a blue cloak spangled with stars, a veil and a golden crown. She indicated with her finger that Jean should kill the lizard, which he did forthwith. The lady smiled, then levitated before disappearing. The boy told his family what he had seen and the news spread rapidly.

Six days later he saw her again; he was accompanied by his brother, sister and a crowd of villagers, but they saw nothing. Jean asked the apparition a favour and, although he would not divulge what it was, claimed later that it had been granted. On a later occasion, he claimed, she told him secrets which he never revealed.

During the next encounter he was followed to the chapel by a light. There he asked Mary if she would cure thirteen-year-old Antoinette Genebrier, a neighbour, who had been deaf since birth. The girl's affliction was eventually cured, which affected her so profoundly that she became a nun.

Testing times

The Virgin now informed Jean that henceforth she would appear on Wednesdays and Saturdays at 11a.m. As the crowds grew, however, Mary appeared to lose her patience. She refused to bless their rosaries and, when set to perform a miracle, cancelled it because people were pushing and shoving. On her ninth appearance, Jean announced that she was weeping. She told him that her son was threatening to punish the villagers by ruining their crops unless they amended their 'sinful' ways. Both this threat and the earlier killing of the lizard do not seem very Christian!

But Jean was not entirely satisfied that the apparition was who she claimed to be. On her eleventh appearance he applied a traditional test, saying: 'If you are the mother of the Lord, step forward. If you are the Devil, step back.' She stepped forward. Then he threw holy water on her; if she had been a demon in disguise she should have disappeared, but the beautiful young woman just smiled.

Jean asked her to create a holy spring, but she gave him an ambiguous answer and it never appeared. By now about eight hundred people were attending the boy's invisible encounters with the Virgin Mary. Her twentieth appearance was the final one.

Although the Church never officially endorsed the experiences, Jean Bernard was educated by them and he became a priest. He died in 1932.

'If you are the mother of the Lord, step forward. If you are the Devil, step back'

THE FATIMA MIRACLES

PERHAPS the most spectacular of these phenomena occurred at the place called Fatima in Portugal in 1917, when two girls began a series of encounters with a radiant lady identified as Mary. Despite the fact that only the girls could see the being, huge crowds began to gather at the events. A series of prophecies was passed on to the girls but some were never made public. It is claimed that the Catholic Church deliberately suppressed them.

A miracle also occurred, which was witnessed by the crowds. At one of the encounters they saw the 'sun' dance across the sky. In the modern age, in a different setting, this would be described as a UFO.

THE GARABANDAL APPARITIONS

DURING the early 1960s in the village of Garabandal in northern Spain four little girls received visions of Michael the Archangel and the Virgin Mary. The genesis of this remarkable phenomenon was recorded in a diary by the main seer, Conchita Gonzalez.

On the evening of 18 June 1961 the four girls were playing in the village square when Conchita and Mari Cruz decided to steal some apples from a tree belonging to their schoolmistress. While eating the illicit apples in a nearby lane they were startled by a noise like thunder. Taking this to be a sign from heaven, Conchita told the others that by their actions they had pleased the Devil and saddened their guardian angels.

While eating stolen apples, the girls were startled by a thunderous noise which they took to be admonition from heaven

Suddenly 'a very beautiful figure that shone brilliantly' appeared before her and she went into ecstasy. The others, Jacinta, Loli and Mari, thought she was having a fit, and were about to fetch Conchita's mother when they too were overtaken by the vision. They identified the figure as the Archangel Michael, who appeared almost daily until Sunday, 2 July.

Conchita described him as looking like a boy of about nine, but with an aura of immense strength and pale rose-coloured wings. He wore a long, flowing blue gown that hid his feet. The entity had a dark complexion and black eyes. On his final appearance the angel spoke to them. According to Conchita's diary, Michael asked them: 'Do you know why I have come? It is to announce that tomorrow, Sunday, the Virgin Mary will appear to you as Our Lady of Mount Carmel.'

The following evening they were on their way to the lane when the

Virgin materialised with an angel on each side of her. There was also a disembodied eye which the girls took to be the eye of God. The Virgin wore a white dress, a blue mantle and a crown of golden stars. She had long dark wavy hair parted in the middle, a long nose and full lips. Her voice was lovely but unique, and difficult for Conchita to describe.

Superhuman abilities

The girls saw the apparitions whilst in a state of altered consciousness, and in this condition their movements were synchronised. There were many witnesses to the girls' remarkable superhuman abilities, some of which were captured on film. They were, for instance, able to bend backwards until their heads touched their waists. In this position they could rush over rocky ground and ditches without losing their footing. The girls could outrun grown men, even when they were running backwards. They could levitate and change their body weight. Miraculous healing also took place.

One of the witnesses to the levitation was former police chief Juan Alvarez Seco, who was interviewed by sceptical researcher and journalist John Cornwell. Brigadier Seco vividly recounted what he witnessed on 28 July 1961 in the kitchen of Conchita's house. With him was Father José Ramon Vasquez, a Dr Ortiz and several other witnesses. Conchita was in ecstasy and begging them to lift her up so she could reach the lips of the Virgin. But when the policeman and two others attempted to lift her they found it impossible. Then one of the other seers, Jacinta, stepped forward and lifted Conchita with the tips of her fingers right up to the ceiling. After kissing the invisible entity Conchita floated back down, with Jacinta just holding on to her legs. After Jacinta let go, for a few moments Conchita remained floating several inches above the kitchen floor.

Father Louis Andreu became closely involved with the girls, and began to share in their visions. But after one visit by the Virgin he dropped down dead. He was only thirty-six years old and no physical reason for his death could be found. Afterwards he continued to speak through the mouths of the girls – not in Spanish, however, but in a variety of 'foreign languages'.

John Cornwell interviewed Conchita's eldest brother, Serafin, and his wife, Pacita. Conchita had told him that during an ecstasy she felt she was 'outside of the world'. A bishop's commission interrogated her and tried to persuade Conchita that it was a collective hallucination. Psychologists and medical doctors became involved too, but no one

The dead priest continued to speak through through the girls' mouths in a variety of languages

could agree on the source of the phenomenon. Serafin told John Cornwell. 'I've seen her in ecstasy running backwards on her knees over razor-sharp rocks, and there wouldn't be a scratch or a mark on her afterwards. Nobody will ever convince me that the phenomena are natural. They *must* be from God.'

Witnesses to a miracle

Pacita was sixteen at the time of the visions, and told how she and many of the other villagers were convinced that they too would see the apparitions. They never did, but they did witness a miracle.

The children often received holy communion with the Archangel. On this occasion Conchita announced to the crowd that the angel would make the host visible on her tongue. People crowded round and stared at the girl's outstretched tongue. They gasped in amazement as the 'host' materialised, 'brilliant and dazzling as snow; it was thicker than the normal host and looked spongy', Pacita explained.

John Cornwell tracked Conchita down in New York where at the age of sixteen she had fled from the publicity and adopted a fresh identity. Cornwell found an attractive thirty-eight-year-old woman who had grave doubts about her past. The Virgin had prophesied a great miracle. A sign would appear over Garabandal, and a date was given which Conchita has never disclosed. She told Cornwell: 'I saw a beautiful lady who told me she was the Blessed Mother. If the miracle doesn't come, then *nothing* is true.'

THE MEDJUGOREJE MIRACLES

THE most popularised, best documented and most scientifically examined case is the one which is still occurring in the village of Medjugoreje in former Yugoslavia. Since 1981, when a group of children started seeing the apparition, over 17 million pilgrims have visited the place.

It began on 24 June when fourteen-year-old Vicka Ivankovic was walking across a field. Suddenly she was confronted by a strange light in the hillside mist. The following day, when the phenomenon reappeared, Ivanka ran and fetched her friends: five other children, their ages ranging from ten to seventeen, joined her. The light resolved into the figure of a woman with long dark hair wearing a grey gown and white veil. She held something in her left hand which she was covering and uncovering. She was identified as the Virgin, and a conversation took place.

From that day onwards the visionaries saw the Virgin regularly and talked with her. The meeting-place was transferred to a room in the village. Others who attended could neither see nor hear anything except the children taking part in what seemed a one-sided 'conversation'. But the children would drop to their knees in perfect coordination.

Vicka Ivankovic. At the age of fourteen, Vicka was one of a group of children to whom the Virgin Mary regularly appeared in the village of Medjugoreje in the former Yugoslavia

Scepticism and antipathy

Initially Father Jozo Zovko, the new parish priest, was sceptical of the alleged phenomena and wondered if the children were lying or mentally ill. He questioned them closely to discover if they were using drugs. He was in the church praying when a voice said to him: 'Go out now and protect the children.' Before he could open the door the children appeared, begging him to save them from the militia: the communist authorities had taken a very dim view of the 'miracles'. Father Jozo hid the children until the search was called off.

Convinced now of the authenticity of the visions, Father Jozo spoke out in their favour. Not only did he have the government to contend with, but also powerful figures within his own religion. In October he was arrested and charged with conspiracy. After eighteen months in prison, on his release Father Jozo was transferred to Tihaljin, some twenty miles from Medjugoreje.

A concrete cross on Mount Krizevac was observed to glow like neon

Scourges on mankind

A cross marks the hillside spot of the original Medjugoreje visions

Soon the trickle of pilgrims had turned into a flood, and at the end of every three- or four-minute encounter the children were debriefed by a Franciscan priest. The phenomena achieved worldwide fame and were even accepted by devout Catholics. Along with the visions there were claims of miracle healings. A concrete cross on Mount Krizevac was observed to glow like neon, and photographs of this phenomenon were taken. But central to all this were the children and their communications with the Virgin Mary.

These communications were mainly concerned with the imparting of ten signs or scourges to be visited on mankind. Before each sign was to appear, the children were instructed to inform a certain priest who would then release the information to the media. But most of the messages were unspectacular, like the following example: 'Dear children! I desire you to be the reflection of Jesus, who enlightens this unfaithful world which is walking in darkness. I wish that all of you be a light to all and to witness in the light. Dear children, you are called to darkness, you are called to light. Therefore, live the light with your life. Thank you for your response to my call.'

Scientific investigations and experiments

In the late 1980s, when John Cornwell visited Medjugoreje and interviewed many of the players in the drama, Vicka Ivankovic, one of the 'children' and now in her twenties, gave him details of the encounters. She described how the Virgin originally came in the form of a 'picture light' before developing into a three-dimensional figure.

> *The Virgin said she was taking them to see heaven, and the three of them began to rise up through the ceiling*

On one occasion the apparition appeared before her and a boy named Jakov, another of the seers, in the boy's house. The Virgin said she was taking them to see heaven. Jakov protested, but she took hold of their hands and the three of them began to rise up through the ceiling, and beyond, until the house had disappeared. They were taken to a place containing 'beautiful flowers and angels'.

Extensive scientific examination of the 'children' was carried out while they were in ecstasy, giving rise to some remarkable results. A team headed by Professor Henri Joyeux of Montpellier University in France conducted a variety of tests which involved the use of electro-encephalographs (machines for taking X-rays of the brain) and electro-oculographs (machines for charting eye movements), as well as eye-reflex tests and examination of evoked auditory responses. The team, which included a brain and ocular surgeon, made five separate visits to Medjugoreje. They wanted to understand why the seers responded in unison to the alleged apparition while their eyes followed her apparent movement; and why, when they talked to her, no sound escaped their lips, even though their larynxes were working. In short, how could the group of young people independently, yet often in unison, react in exactly the same way that they would react to a real person standing before them?

The results of the tests indicate that the seers were not in a state of altered consciousness, which would rule out the sceptics' favourite theory of temporal lobe epilepsy. The coordinated movement of the children was thought by some to be the result of them consciously or unconsciously picking up cues from one dominant member of the group. But not all members of the group were together on every occasion, and the various combinations did not seem to make any difference. Their responses were within 0.1 and 0.4 of a second. Electro-oculograms showed that the eyes of the seers all responded at the same moment when the apparition first appeared. Psychological examinations could find no neuroses or psychoses. Psychological testing by Professor Cadilhac showed the subjects to be of average intelligence.

Before the scientific studies began, the tests were crude. On one occasion a priest armed with an unsterilised needle stabbed one of the girls through her clothing whilst she was in communication with the Virgin. She did not appear to experience any pain. Italian scientists Dr Farina and Professor Santini were more sophisticated and used an algometer to measure the seers' sensitivity to pain. This electronic instrument calibrates a subject's reaction to being touched with a hot piece of metal. Under normal conditions the seers reacted as quickly as anyone else to the heat – between 0.3 and 0.4 of a second. However, during an encounter none of them registered pain. Heat was applied to them for seven seconds, and then stopped to avoid burning them badly.

When a priest stabbed one of the girls with an unsterilised needle to test her, she felt no pain

Dr Santini discovered that during ecstasy the subjects' eyes displayed none of the normal reactions to stimulus. Using an estesiometer, a device that measures corneal response, he found that no reflex was registered at all. The eyes could not be stimulated to blink or cry, and the pupil did not contract when confronted with a very bright light. The scientists were able to ascertain that stimulus was being conveyed to the brain – but there, in the cortex, it was blocked.

Environmental factors were studied by nuclear physicist Professor Emmanual More and electro-chemist Paul Ameze. They found only normal background radiation.

Now the Medjugoreje visions are the subject of a major film starring Martin Sheen, Morgan Fairchild and Michael York. Sheen plays the part of Father Jozo.

MOTHER OF CHRIST OR IMPOSTER?

MEDJUGOREJE has provided scientists with a unique opportunity to test visionaries for a prosaic explanation, yet those 'explanations' have been found wanting. There have been over 230 major recorded encounters with the Virgin Mary during the twentieth century. Should we be prepared to take these visions at face value? Is the Virgin Mary really visiting children from her home in heaven?

It is interesting that to begin with the apparition never identifies itself as the Virgin Mary. Indeed, in some cases the phenomenon first appears as a strange light. It is the percipients who conclude that it is the Virgin; then the vision obligingly takes on that role.

Why are percipients of Mary always children? Is it because they are more receptive to the paranormal because they have not yet been taught what is 'possible' and what is 'impossible'? Adults become socialised, indeed indoctrinated, with cultural beliefs, whereas children are more open to eccentric ideas – wherever they might come from.

And if these visions really are the mother of Christ, why preach to the converted and appear only before peasants in Catholic countries? Scientific testing has demonstrated that the visions are not ordinary hallucinations, there really is something there. But what is it, and where is it from?

It is the percipients who conclude that the phenomenon is the Virgin, after which the vision takes on that role

MARY'S MESSAGES

At face value the purpose of the encounters is to renew faith in God and reinforce a code of behaviour which will benefit society and save the world from destruction. In that respect the messages given to the percipients have been mundane and repetitive. Critics, looking for proof of the authenticity of the entity, have waited in vain. Mary is not prepared to add historical detail to the biblical story which scholars could verify.

In 1991 an American nurse, Annie Kirkwood, published the results of her encounters with the Virgin. Annie does not receive visions, but 'hears' Mary talking to her. Annie is not Catholic and at first argued with the voice, but was finally convinced that she should be the mouthpiece for the mother of Christ.

Mary told her that she had appeared to many people over the last two hundred years in an attempt to avert our civilisation from catastrophe. As a spiritual being she could appear in several places at once. Annie was informed that many natural disasters were to be visited on mankind. This was not punishment from God, but the results of our abuse of the earth.

Mary made some predictions which included earthquakes and volcanic eruptions during the 1990s. These appear to have been remarkably accurate, but since the events they forefold took place before the publication of Annie Kirkwood's book the authenticity of the predictions is not verifiable.

The book describes how weather conditions would become so

The Virgin told the American nurse that as a spiritual being she could appear in several places at once extreme that many people would become convinced that the world was in its last days. That was to happen in 1993 but, as we know, it never came about. It was also claimed that New York would be flooded in 1994, forcing a permanent evacuation. For 1995, it was predicted that a giant earthquake would cause California to disappear beneath the sea. Towards the end of that year the earth would begin to move on its axis. None of these events have occurred.

Despite this, Mary was accurate in describing devastating earthquakes in Japan, but sceptics will say that anyone who makes random predictions will strike lucky some of the time. Annie Kirkwood said she was loath to publish the predictions in case they were wrong, but the entity insisted, telling her: 'Understand that these predictions can be alleviated and lessened with prayer. Pray for the people of the world to turn to God the Father.'

Sceptics will view this as a handy escape clause. Messages from heaven? From the mind? Or from mischievous entities?

Chapter 9

THE GATES
OF PARADISE

I N THE first half of this book, we have looked at a wide range of evidence to suggest that there could be survival in some sort of afterlife. Now we must change the emphasis and enter territory that is less soundly based on scientific discussion and is rooted firmly in belief and expectation. We will examine what we term 'postcards from heaven' – information transmitted by the mind, often via mediums, and allegedly coming from those who have passed through death and yet 'live on' in this apparent afterlife. Such information is difficult to evaluate, but is essential to provide a full picture. So, whilst we offer no guarantees about the nature of the evidence you will confront in the next few chapters, it is wise to bear in mind that many thousands, perhaps even millions, of people claim to receive these postcards from heaven. No doubt those recipients would ask us to ponder – can they all be wrong?

*W*HAT IS IT LIKE TO DIE?

This is not a question that many of us will dwell upon until we are faced with that terrible prospect in our own life. Then we may square up to it, perhaps for the first time, and realise with shock that it is an omission in our years of education.

At school we learn about wars fought centuries ago where relevance seems obscure. But every child must one day face death – be it their own, or that of someone who is close to them. Indeed, it could happen

The good being welcomed to the kingdom of heaven. A detail from a painting by Rogier van der Weyden (1399-1464)

whilst they are still at school. The March 1996 massacre of five-year-olds in a Scottish primary school was an almost incomprehensible tragedy. Yet the mental scars on the survivors are made much worse because our society treats death as an issue that no child should think about. Jenny Randles describes her own experiences in this unspoken territory. We suspect that they are typical of those of many readers.

FINAL MOMENTS: A PERSONAL EXPERIENCE

The trauma of the grandmother's sudden death and a vivid OOBE just before the funeral nearly caused a nervous breakdown

'THE first time that I came across death was in 1971 at the age of nineteen. My maternal grandmother died suddenly when staying at our house in Manchester. I was very close to her, and her death after a brief illness cut deep. I was at university and was so traumatised by the experience that I virtually dropped out. As a result of this trauma and a vivid OOBE just before the funeral I suspect I may have come close to a nervous breakdown.

'My grandmother's death knocked me sideways because nobody had prepared me for it. Indeed, my grandmother seems to have been more prepared than I was. The day before her death she must have known that her time was limited and told me that I should have one of her precious possessions. When the doctor came early that morning to see her through her final moments I stood dumbstruck, too shocked to be sad, and watched her stare intently from the sick bed that had been set up in our living room. Her gaze was fixed on the kitchen door and she was cheerfully talking to people whom she obviously knew well. I looked into the space, trying to figure out who she could see and I could not. Then she just slipped away.

Nobody had told me what death was like. I asked what had just happened and was told that she had seen her own parents who had taken her to heaven, or – according to the doctor – that she was hallucinating because of her illness (he had not given her any painkillers so this was not a factor). Whatever the truth, I knew that death was not the simple expiration I expected it to be.

'Twenty-four years later my father died. Near the end he started to have minor, yet clear-cut, psychic experiences such as a vivid precognition of a football match – one of his true loves. He was the most sceptical, least psychic person I have ever met, so these events were all the more startling. It was as if he were already halfway into the next world.'

TRANSITIONS

ALL those who have faced death from this side of life in the way Jenny Randles has just described it will appreciate the word used by Spiritualists. When one of their number dies they do not utter bland euphemisms like 'passed on'. Instead they say the person has been 'promoted', for they think of the afterlife as a step up in the long ladder of spiritual evolution.

Norman Goodman of the Longsight Spiritualist Church in Manchester has had contact with many people who have been promoted from this world and describes it in these words: 'Death is not the end. There is no death at all. We just start the second part of our life in the spirit world and progress on that side.'

This theme of a gradual transition from one phase of existence to the other, via the gateway into heaven, is the ethos of all beliefs formed out of contacts from the afterlife. It also matches well the experience of dying as seen from the only side of the mirror through which most of us can view it.

'There is no death at all. We just start the second part of our life in the spirit world and progress on that side'

'But why?'

American comedian Sam Kinison died as a result of a terrible car crash in Las Vegas in 1992. Crawling from the remains of his pick-up after a head-on collision, he seemed to have superficial injuries but was in fact dying. Eye-witnesses who rushed to the scene urged him to take it easy, but he was frantically pleading into thin air that he did not want to die. It soon became evident that he was having an animated conversation with some unseen person, which gradually subsided to the words 'But why?' The startled onlookers then heard him say 'Okay' resignedly several times – the last time extremely softly. He then died from internal injuries and shock. Those who watched these final moments were sure he was in conversation with someone 'on the other side' who assured him it was time to move on.

This case makes a fascinating contrast with the accounts in Chapter 4 of NDE witnesses who alleged that they were given a choice by discarnate entities when they were hovering in limbo between life and death. Of course, they all opted to live on – which is why they came back and we got to hear their stories. Does Sam Kinison's passing give us an insight into what happens when the person eventually decides not to return?

WELCOME TO HEAVEN

*A*s we saw earlier, those who return after an NDE often allege that they encountered dead relatives who sent them back to earth. This concept of being met on arrival at the gates of heaven seems to be one of the most commonly reported in the countless messages that come from the afterlife.

Similar information is offered about this type of meeting from both mediums – according to their alleged communications with the dead – as well as from their spirit guides (see p. 45), supposedly speaking about one's arrival in heaven from their more lofty perspective. Many guides, as explained earlier, are from cultures which pay (or paid) great attention to psychic matters.

These guides are in some sense the equivalent of a medium operating on the 'other side'. They claim to be psychically and spiritually gifted and so find it easier to communicate with earth. However, they do not only pass their messages through traditional mediums. There are also what are known as 'channelers' – through whom these guides speak verbally, convey philosophy and even write extensive volumes about the nature of the heavenly realm. A good example is Gildas (pronounced Jill-das) who professes to be a medieval monk from the Provençal region of France. He has for many years sent messages through the voice of Englishwoman, Ruth White. She considers him an external entity and says that she does not always agree with his teachings. At first she pictured him in white robes. Now she claims to see him in a refined spirit body, glowing with many colours. Gildas claims that Ruth is his earthly twin and that they are bonded spiritually across eternity. He explains that communications from the afterlife can sometimes be difficult because the earth is material and time-dependent, whereas these are concepts difficult to grasp when you have been out-of-the-body for centuries.

The teachings of spirit guides are very influential in many people's beliefs about life after death. Do they offer consistent accounts of what it is like to pass over?

Making adjustments

One of the most respected guides in Spiritualist circles is Silver Birch. There are many books filled with the communications that have supposedly been passed on by him through various mediums, although his existence on earth has never been historically established. Death, he tells us, comes about when the tie between our spirit (or etheric) body and the physical body within the material world severs, whether gradually or suddenly.

In physical birth the spirit enters the body, and in physical death it leaves to return home

---

'Physical death is equivalent to physical birth,' he says. In the latter case the spirit enters the body, and in the former it leaves to return home. Although death itself is painless, traumas may result if the body is ill during transition. Doctors in the spirit world greet new arrivals and take over from their earth-bound equivalents. Otherwise it can be difficult to adjust to the new world. A period of rest, similar to a long sleep, is said to follow in such circumstances. The same is true when someone dies who is very materially minded or atheistic and would simply get too great a shock at suddenly awakening into a new state for which they were mentally unprepared.

On the other hand, 'those with knowledge have no such problems,' the guide tells us. 'They step out of the world of matter into the world of spirit. ... It is a moment of supreme joy because it brings recognition of all the loved ones who have been waiting for [the transition] to occur.'

Growing older, growing younger

In a sitting with Jenny Randles, Lancashire medium Hilda Totty contacted the spirit of a baby that had been miscarried by a woman who was also present. This had taken place exactly one year earlier and only the woman knew about this miscarriage – until the medium announced the fact!

This unborn baby had entered the spirit world, Hilda said, and been cared for in a rest facility by deceased relatives. She could communicate with it because 'the power of the mind grows so quickly in the next stage of life. Infants grow and reach maturity as they would have done had they been allowed to live in a physical body. A baby under a year of age can reach twenty-two, twenty-three or even thirty in a very short space of time.'

Indeed, according to other messages from the afterlife the same applies in reverse to older people. They gradually grow younger in the afterlife until they take on the optimum age of between thirty-five and forty – at least in so far as they are perceived by other inhabitants of the spirit world. This is slightly older than other sources claim.

THE BIG SLEEP

BRITISH Spiritualist priest, Brother John, a noted commentator for *Psychic News* for many years, explains that stressful physical ailments can occur when the brain in the material body is unable to keep up with the

British Spiritualist priest, Brother John

undamaged communications from its eternally healthy spirit partner. 'On passing to the spirit world the physical brain and its deficiencies are left behind. There may be the necessity for a period of rest and readjustment before the etheric brain becomes active again; but as it does, so does memory. All that is of importance concerned with earth life has been stored and is available to the now mentally sound soul.'

The Exeter Spiritualist Church in Devon even claims to have tuned in to the setting up of one of these rest homes in the afterlife, in conjunction with a highly experienced medical director. Michael Evans spoke of contact with a woman who died after a long bout of rheumatism and on arrival in heaven needed the big sleep to prepare her to move on. After awakening in a spirit clinic she discovered its value and became the founder of a new centre to greet arrivals with similar problems. Working in conjunction with her was Florence Nightingale. It seems that the founder of the nursing movement had been susceptible to assistance from the spirit world during her pioneering medical work on earth. Only after her death did she understand the nature of this help, and she was now using her talents by easing into the afterlife those whom medicine still could not protect.

Florence Nightingale acknowledged assistance from the spirit world while she was nursing on the earthly plane

George Meek, whom we met earlier in connection with his work in the field of electronic contact with the dead, has received many messages from the afterlife via his equipment. He explained that we gradually emigrate to heaven even before we actually die. 'For some months or even years before their minds and souls made the final transition [very sick people] were in fact spending time on short visits to their next plane of life.' This, Meck says, may

Spiritualists in Devon claim to have received information that Florence Nightingale is actively involved in caring for new arrivals in rest homes in the afterlife

help explain the absent expression often reported in the eyes of people just before death – or indeed the sudden spurt of psychic abilities observed in Jenny Randles' father in his final days.

LIFE IN THE WORLD UNSEEN

POSSIBLY the most famous account of the actual transfer between lives comes in Anthony Borgia's *Life in the World Unseen*. This book is supposedly based upon spirit messages received from a Roman Catholic priest, Monsignor Robert Benson, during the years following his death in 1914. They were conveyed to Borgia by way of automatic writing. This process involves the spirit entity reputedly taking over the hands of the medium or channel whilst they are in an altered state of consciousness and using them to write out the thoughts or messages that the guide wishes to convey. The writing appears to come automatically – hence the term – although sceptics argue that the source is just as likely to be the deep subconscious of the medium, rather than a being who exists in some life-after-death state.

Benson tells of how several times in the days before his death the priest experienced a 'feeling of floating away and of gently returning', which appear to be references to an out-of-body state. His mind was lucid. He knew he was going to die and he was eager to make the transition. Suddenly, he had 'a great urge to rise up'. He felt as if he was in a very lucid dream, aware of what was happening but without physical sensation. Nobody at his deathbed noticed that he had got up.

> *'I saw my physical body lying lifeless upon its bed, but here was I, the real I, alive and well'*

'Turning, I then beheld what had taken place,' he reports. 'I saw my physical body lying lifeless upon its bed, but here was I, the *real* I, alive and well.' The priest was aware of the room and its occupants, even though a misty light partially filled it. He was surprised to see that his spirit body was wearing clothes that he might have put on to potter about the house.

Perhaps the most curious aspect of this account is that Benson does not describe being out of the body from an elevated position, in the way of virtually every OOBE otherwise recorded, but seemed to be standing as if on the floor. It is, however, possible that he simply omitted mention of perspective.

This process of awakening took only a few minutes, but it was not until his self-appraisal of his after-death state was complete that Benson realised he had been joined by another spirit form. Unlike the grieving relatives surrounding the bed, this person was well able to see him. It was a priest whom he had known well, but who had died some time before. They allegedly communicated with one another 'just as we had always done upon the earth – that is, we simply used our vocal cords and spoke quite as a matter of course'.

The new arrival told Benson that he would take him to his new home. Because of his illness, it was said, he would need the big sleep and so it was not advisable to walk to heaven. Benson was urged to hold tight and close his eyes, and then felt himself floating upwards. After a while the priest felt something solid beneath his feet. Opening his eyes once more, he found that they had arrived in a spirit re-creation of his old home, apparently chosen to ease the transition and allow him to familiarise himself with the new world.

It is impossible to know if Borgia's words truly reflect an account of someone's arrival in the spirit world or simply stem from imagination and wishful thinking. But it certainly reflects the tales told by many others who are allegedly communicating from this life after death.

THE ACT OF DEATH

WE can perhaps now combine our 'knowledge' from a variety of sources and present a portrait of a typical experience of the act of death.

Loosening the bonds

During the latter stages of an illness the ties between the earthly body and the spirit seem to loosen. This can be experienced by the dying person as out-of-body states, lucid dreams, images of dead loved ones and even flashes of ESP (extra-sensory perception). Witnesses on earth may also sense this gradual withdrawal from the body, and if they are particularly sensitive may even experience more dramatic things at the point of death. This could range from simple awareness of the moment of passing, for instance in a dream or as an intuition, to a visual observation of the spirit departing the body or even an image of the dead person seeming to pause on the way to heaven with a message for their family.

If death occurs through illness, the transfer may occur in an unconscious state. As a result little is evident either to those looking on or to the person who is dying. This is perhaps the most common way of going. The out-of-body state seems to be experienced more often if a violent event such as a sudden accident is the cause of death. The person finds themselves floating free and aware that their real self is now somehow apart from the physical body, which may be mangled in the wreckage of a car or lying on an operating table below. Yet it is viewed as completely detached and irrelevant.

The frequently described tunnel effect and passage towards a bright light may be a hallucinatory product of stresses in the physical body. Similar reports appear in circumstances far removed from any possibility of life after death, such as during alleged kidnap by aliens. This seems to imply that these features of the NDE are related more to physical processes within the brain than to any transition to a life after death. Does this account for the absence of tunnel imagery in most stories of the transition as communicated to us direct from those supposedly in the afterlife?

The OOBE does, however, crop up in many accounts from the after-life and, as we saw in Chapter 4, is frequently present in NDE reports. This may genuinely reflect the spirit or etheric body rising up from the physical body as the bonds are loosened or broken.

The transfer into the after-death environment is often vividly described by NDE witnesses, but is generally less well recalled in the many messages sent to us from residents in heaven. Perhaps this is because the long sleep is so often required for recuperative purposes, and memory is blurred after awakening.

It may be that the sensation of moving upwards and the diffuse light said to permeate the afterlife, both described in typical NDE stories, are made more dramatic in such cases because of the swiftness of the passing and the fact that the brain remains alive throughout. Could it be that these experiences become progressively more mystical and hard to express in our mundane, logical terms once the physical body is no longer available for possible return? Does this explain why postcards from heaven seem so different from NDE experiences?

The sensation of passing through a tunnel towards a bright light may be a hallucination caused by stresses in the dying physical body

A CHANGE OF APPAREL

THE next most common reference is to being greeted by a loved one and helped into the afterlife. This is so typical that there is hardly any case among the hundreds of communications from heaven that we have studied whilst compiling this book where it is not reported. The same feature is also found in some NDEs – usually those where the victims travel furthest towards death.

Possibly this meeting is one of the final events at the ultimate barrier between the two worlds. Once you encounter these dead relatives, you either return swiftly to earth or you agree to go on with them and enter the bright light which is heaven. Then you are ready to face the next great adventure that supposedly awaits you.

American psychic Mabel Rowland expressed all this in her own terms for a 1942 account of the transition which she called *How to Die*. She said, 'We awaken in the next state of existence, discovering that our thought and feeling reactions are exactly the same as they always were. Remember that. You are *you*. There is no death. There is only a change of apparel, so to speak.'

Chapter 10

A NEW WORLD

LOCATING heaven is far from easy. Despite what earlier cultures thought you cannot find it in any atlas, and astronomers have never been able to send back photographs from probes rocketed towards the furthest corners of the universe. If the afterlife is a real place, where is it?

FINDING HEAVEN?

BROTHER John reminds us that Spiritualist teachings say that after you die you do not actually travel anywhere; heaven should be considered a realm or dimension that constantly penetrates our physical world. In other words, we do not go up or down, east or west, in the normal spatial sense, but shift frequency vibrations in a way that modern science has yet to appreciate fully.

This gives the curious image of the dead not really having left at all. They may be around us all of the time but we are simply unable to perceive them – just as, it is claimed, they cannot ordinarily witness us without making a particular effort to do so.

Following the laws of physics

Fantastic though this may sound, it is not wildly out of step with modern physics. If you take a lump of ice and put it on a table, it is perfectly visible for what it is. As time passes the ice melts to become a liquid, water, which can flow anywhere. The energy picked up from heat in the room has caused the atoms in the ice to vibrate faster and so completely change its state.

The analogy becomes even more apt if we add further heat to the room, when something yet more intriguing takes place. The water disappears and we see nothing at all. In effect, we might argue, the water has vanished. In fact, the same law of physics has made the atoms vibrate faster still to turn the water into a gas which it is impossible for our normal senses to detect.

But the existence of this gas is evidenced by the sudden appearance shortly afterwards of a film of water on a cool glass surface such as a mirror on the far side of the room. This is the same water that was visible before, formed from identical atoms. It has been brought back into our awareness because it has transferred some heat to the surface of the mirror and in the process reduced its frequency again. We say that the gas has now condensed into a liquid.

It is not difficult to think here in terms of a visible entity (the ice block) gradually breaking down (or dying) in front of our eyes and finally disappearing altogether (to become the deceased person). To us it has gone, perhaps never to be seen again. Yet, suddenly an ethereal watery form seems to be manifesting in the cooler parts of the room. Has a ghost of the ice block returned to haunt us? No – it is simply a matter of the application of physics and the limitations of our human senses. The ice never really went away, of course – it was simply out of our range of perception for a time, although we could have developed measuring instruments to prove that it was still there. Is this just what mediums do – allow us to view what has become temporarily invisible?

A HOME AWAY FROM HOME

The various concepts of the afterlife have some elements in common but there are often subtle differences. Ideas from a number of mediums and similar sources are given below, followed by a more general description of the Spiritualist view of heaven (see p. 125).

Jenny Randles first asked famous British medium Doris Collins how she perceives the afterlife. Mediums find that conditions are apparently so similar to those they have left behind on earth that many who have passed over need to be convinced that they are really dead. 'We pass to a state that we have an understanding of,' Doris explained. The kind of

'The kind of environment we enter after death is dictated by the life that we have led and the way in which we utilise the gifts that we have been given'

environment we enter after death is dictated by the life that we have led and the way in which we utilise the gifts that we have been given.'

Doris added that people find themselves in an afterlife whose surroundings depend to a considerable degree upon their own mental perception and are forged to a large extent out of the acts they have performed throughout their life. In other words, if we are kind, then we reap our reward by awakening in a more beautiful abode that we would do if our lives were more self-centred.

However, this image of a very earthly heaven (which is an extremely consistent feature of post-mortal communications) does lead to some apparent absurdities. Earlier we heard of Florence Nightingale running a hostel to welcome sick people who have recently died. But can there really be a Hollywood in heaven?

An American medium claims that comedians Bud Abbott and Lou Costello have produced sixty-four movies in heaven

---

That is the claim of a medium in the American journal *Voices from Spirit*. He says that the two great film comedians Bud Abbott and Lou Costello, who died many years ago, have been in contact from their new abode and had by 1993 produced sixty-four movies in heaven. Now they are looking for earthbound sponsors to bring their work to a living audience! Elsewhere we have been told that Marshal Wyatt Earp has written a novel and that the baseball star Babe Ruth is still hitting home runs in the league of dead all-stars. Somewhere along the line you do have to wonder where vivid imagination ends and genuine communication begins.

A THINKING PERSON'S GUIDE TO THE AFTERLIFE

ACCORDING to automatic writing medium Jane Sherwood, at death 'one finds oneself in a fantastic dream world with no continuity of experience'. This only stabilises into some sort of order when the dead person accepts their new condition. However, even then thought seems to rule the universe.

An American medium claims to be in contact with the great film comedians Abbott (left) and Costello.
They have apparently made sixty-four movies in heaven!

'Lincoln' is one of the most extraordinary channels in modern British Spiritualism. This young man claims to be a physical medium, conjuring up seemingly living, three-dimensional images from the dead who regularly communicate through him. This is done during a trance by extracting from his body a white, softly flowing substance called ectoplasm which is normally unseen and etheric in nature. The spirit shapes a physical form out of this material, rather as we might mould an image from within our heads using clay or plasticine.

Doubts have been raised about the authenticity of such astonishing spiritual comebacks, carried out in darkened rooms where testing is difficult and photography impossible. But Lincoln has many supporters from those who have sat with him, notably amongst the Noah's Ark Society which specialises in this type of work.

One of Lincoln's guides, Daphne, is a dead woman who serves as his support in the spirit world and often reveals information about the afterlife. Psychic research journalist Tim Haigh described one such sitting in early 1992 at which Daphne appeared and discussed her new life.

According to Daphne's word the first level of heaven, often called the first astral plane, is a world 'made up of images projected from our own minds'. It is a thought-produced heaven, which fits the environment on earth with which we have become most familiar during our lives, because that is how our post-death consciousness is bound to picture it. All thought stems from experience, and our earth world is the most vivid experience shared by the newly arriving dead.

The first level of heaven is a world 'made up of images projected from our own minds'

Mark Macey of Continuing Life Research in the USA also confirms this picture and explains that from the instrumental messages (ie the messages received via radio, TV and so on) that his team receive from the afterlife this world becomes very clear. 'People and places in the astral plane are real and they do look very like people and places here on earth. Fourteen million people die each day. They carry along with them into the spirit worlds their memories and expectations. Since the chief rule or law in the spirit worlds is 'Thoughts create reality', the people arriving from earth actually create these spirit worlds and communities with their memories and expectations.'

How far we can reasonably take such a position? If you believed you only had one leg because it had been amputated surely your spirit self would have only one leg? Yet according to nearly all spirit communications the physical body is instantly made whole again after death. How does this square up?

These messages suggest that the afterlife is a gigantic illusion or shared hallucination, made real because so many people believe in it.

'Lincoln' is a physical medium who is seemingly able to conjure up living, three-dimensional images from the dead

The form depends upon the mental patterns that the discarnate spirits bring with them beyond death. No doubt in this way heaven must also be full of new housing developments, the latest Japanese technology and a constantly changing moral climate. This leaves a rather disquieting impression of life after death which is filled with the problems, disadvantages and mistakes so commonly found on earth.

MANY MANSIONS

'In my Father's house are many mansions,' runs a famous biblical quotation from Jesus which has often been appropriated by believers in life after death. Does it describe heaven? As an allegory it may be quite accurate, if one accepts the messages from the spirit world. All are agreed on one thing – that the first place we enter after death is but a starting point and we progress onward and upward into other spheres or dimensions.

In his lengthy automatic writings, as given to Anthony Borgia, the spirit form of Monsignor Robert Benson explained the make-up of these heavenly realms. The first point of contact he had was within his own bedroom, implying that here the spirit world directly penetrated our own physical realm. Yet mediums tell us that it is just as difficult for people in spirit to see earth as it is for them to view these disembodied entities. So how could Benson (and his friend who came to meet him) seemingly linger in this earthly place witnessing all that went on around them? One clue offered by Benson is that just after death the spirit is closer to earth than it will ever be again, perhaps as the transition settles down and whilst the physical world is so fresh in the mind.

An example of automatic writing from the notebooks of former clergyman and medium Stainton Moses (late nineteenth century)

When the priest who greeted Benson moved him onward he learned that there were various dimensions to heaven, numbered from one (the closest to earth) to seven (the most refined and spiritual). This is supposedly the origin of the term 'seventh heaven' which many people use, unaware that they are supporting a belief in Spiritualist survival. According to Benson these spheres are 'ranged in a series of bands forming a number of concentric circles around the earth. These circles reach out into the infinity of space.'

Messages from the afterlife contain a lot of conflicting evidence

He adds (in complete contradiction to the Vidicom image of planet Marduk and its three warming suns) that 'the sun has no influence whatever upon the spirit world. We have no consciousness of it at all since it is purely material.' This is just one of several glaring conflicts of evidence about the afterlife in these messages from beyond.

Benson appears not to have gone to the first heaven, usually referred to as 'the lower realms', which is populated by ultra-materialistic people who are so close to earth when they die that they do not want to give up its physical status. There are also higher realms towards which one may aspire by spiritual progress. It is not possible, without special effort, to change realms, although temporary journeys do seem to occur.

According to these scripts, each of the seven heavens comprises a gradation. At the very lowest levels of the first realm are evil, wicked people who wallow in their own misdeeds. Benson painted a picture of a trip down into this close approximation of hell – the beautiful, flower-filled landscape deteriorating into barren rock and the light fading into grey, murky darkness. At the base, all is dark and beings in ragged scraps of clothing struggle across a steaming, volcano-strewn terrain. They will only move out of here, Benson was told, when they themselves choose to do so by improving their spiritual worth – not that they seem to have much chance of that in such a place.

Medium Doris Collins also described this lower realm to us. She explained that each individual enters a niche within heaven that their life on earth has prepared for them. Wicked and evil people, or those obsessed with greed and self-importance, create a landscape of horror by their own actions. In other words, hell is very much of our own making.

Meek's Spiricom sources, too, describe a series of realms. He refers to nine of them, although there are three sub-divisions of the seventh heaven which might be considered as one. It would thus appear that there is not a great discrepancy between the Meek and Borgia geographies of heaven.

Flying the Astral Planes

A brief review of these various and somewhat confusing realms would seem appropriate. However, the descriptions below should not be regarded as more than a guide. There are many areas of dispute amongst the messages from the afterlife and what follows is merely an attempt to combine some of the more consistent reports.

First heaven

The first heaven, or lower astral plane, is the hell-like world of purgatory and self-recrimination from which escape is very slow and difficult. It may take hundreds of years of earth time for its inhabitants to accept their misdeeds, put them right and move upward. Here you would find criminals and materially-obsessed individuals. We are told that the demons and poltergeists which readily interfere with life on earth originate here. The 'bad' parts of heaven are the closest to earth, which explains why religion wrongly equates the occult as a pact with the Devil. Messages on ouija boards, for instance, often come from troubled souls in these near-earth realms.

Second heaven

Most people who die initially find themselves in the second heaven or intermediate astral planes. Viewed as a sort of resting point on the way from earth to the more rarified upper dimensions, it is the thought-created universe that we learned about on p. 119 – the one that closely resembles an idealised earth. Its inhabitants seem to live in physical bodies, wear clothes and so forth – but of an etheric kind that would be invisible on earth. Most attempts to communicate from heaven stem from here; but because its inhabitants are as yet unfamiliar with the afterlife these communications can be confusing or wrong.

Third heaven

The third heaven or higher astral realm is referred to by Spiritualists as 'summerland', for it is the closest thing to the Christian concept of paradise. The most inspired and pure souls from earth pass directly here after death; most people, however, must strive to reach it after a sojourn in the realm below, where they assess their life on earth and try to understand what they did wrong. It is from the third heaven that rebirth back on earth supposedly occurs – although the decision to go back and try again is allegedly an individual one, and some may opt to forsake material life altogether and move into the higher spiritual realms. Some of the best (that is, accurate) and most inspirational messages received via mediums are said to originate here. This may also be the place called Marduk according to the messages received by Vidicom researchers.

Fourth heaven

In the fourth heaven (which Meek refers to as the mental and causal planes) most of the trappings of materialism have gone. It is here that selfless individuals work together to bring spiritual enlightenment to the lower slopes of heaven and to earth. Supposedly all great inventions, religious and moral progressions, spiritual leadership and so on come from here, inspired by beings who were once on earth but have had the opportunity to increase their talents in the afterlife. A few rebirths to earth do take place from this higher plane: great teachers are sent back for special reasons. Spirit guides who talk through mediums are often in this realm as well, bringing their enhanced knowledge to earth.

The fifth heaven is aspired to by great religious figures such as Buddha and Jesus Christ

Fifth heaven

Reaching the fifth or celestial heaven is difficult, for it is devoid of physical state and aspired to by great religious figures, from Jesus to Buddha. Even those in lower heavenly regions view it as most of us still on earth imagine heaven – a distant, magical, unknown place.

Sixth heaven

The sixth heaven is cosmic consciousness, where the unity of souls is perfected and a kind of universal being exists. This may be close to what we think of as God, but it is even less understood by those on the lower astral planes.

Seventh heaven

To reach the seventh heaven one has to step not only beyond material and physical reality but beyond mental and individual reality as well. It is simply not possible to define what this ultimate level may be, but it is supposedly the goal of all individual souls. Everything that we do, on earth and in heaven, is directed towards that final transformation. For there is evolution of the soul in just the same way as there is evolution of the body, or indeed of all life, back on earth.

More things in heaven

Many messages have come through to earth about life in the second heaven. Below are a series of typical questions that have been posed, together with the responses of various post-mortal commentators. None of these claims is necessarily endorsed by the authors of this book: we are merely reflecting what the messages convey.

Are there animals?

Yes, says almost every source. Noted scientist Sir Oliver Lodge (insisting that he was no longer a 'Sir' as there are no titles in the afterlife) explained that 'in very low forms of mind, law and order can be divided into many parts. But as we go through the evolution of mind and body there appears to be a stage when mind has gathered around itself so many layers of emotion, reason and intellect that we deserve to retain our individuality.'

What he means is that every form of life evolves, physically and spiritually, both on earth and then in heaven. However, basic life-forms such as algae, grass or lower animals have a very long way to progress as yet. Most animal species have group souls, and one individual is part of a large collection. Upon death it returns here like a drop of rain falling into the sea, having originated as water vapour rising.

If you cut up an earthworm several new creatures can seem to form, because each is part of the group soul. Some species such as ants, termites and bees act and think as if they were a group rather than as individuals. Spiritualist teachings say this is a general principle and even human beings show some signs – witness the behaviour of crowds.

Spiritualist Maurice Barnabell took a particular interest in the subject. It is argued that pet animals grow spiritually and, whilst still part of the group soul, may have an etheric body that we could meet in heaven. We have, in effect, aided in their spiritual development by way of our love for them. However, any meeting would occur largely through our intervention, not because it is part of the pet's individual progression.

Little is known about very intelligent creatures such as dolphins, but it is worth noting that the messages clearly state that man is not the most advanced being. Our earthly supremacy is an illusion. There are in fact beings from higher levels than the second heaven which inhabit earth in such a way that only rarely do we experience them this side of death. Fairies and angels are supposedly in this category.

Messages from the afterlife clearly state that man is not the most advanced being

Do we need to eat?

Most messages tell us that, as food provides energy, it is no longer necessary when there are no organs to fuel. However, one woman told us that her dead husband had returned in a dream and informed her that there were plenty of supermarkets in heaven! This seems to clash with the lack of a requirement to eat, and the absence of money and material wealth of any kind, which are also commonly alleged by communicants. Indeed, food is one of the biggest sources of discrepancy in the various messages.

Meek asserts from his Spiricom sources that there is no food. 'The higher, finer, vibratory bodies in the worlds of spirit can draw all needed energies directly from the cosmos.' But an Italian called Franchezzo gave a detailed account of a banquet that he attended in heaven, noting: 'Do you imagine that a spirit has no need for food of any kind? If so, you are in error. We need, and we eat, food, though not of so material a substance as is yours.' There is wonderful fruit, Franchezzo adds, that melts in the mouth, and wine like nectar. However, he claims that in the lower realms the earth-besotted spirits take living bodies so as to experience the pleasures of real food again. You may also recall the man from Bradford who claimed to have visited heaven whilst in a coma and to have seen people fighting for scraps of food on the rocky floors in these lower realms.

Of course, it could simply be that food can be 'thought' into existence by those who find it hard to do without one of their greatest pleasures on earth. And if, as Meek says, it is not actually necessary those who feel the pull of the earth plane less can dispense with it altogether.

Is there sex after death?

John Lennon, returning from the afterlife via California medium Bill Tenuto, stated that sex was possible. Some unevolved souls took over earth bodies (perhaps the source of all those ghostly sexual possession stories). But sex in heaven was not as we knew it.

Spiritualist Brother John adds: 'As I understand it sex does exist in the spirit world, but the desires which on earth accompanied it are changed.' He talks of a 'union of the soul … a form of sex on a higher moral scale' and notes the terrible suffering that must be endured on the lower astral planes by sex perverts and criminals who take their urges beyond death but are now unable to fulfil them. If they try to find a way to live out these tendencies, it may provoke the sort of demonic possession that many religions fear.

In assessing the messages via Spiricom George Meek points out that people who were close on earth tend to stay spiritually bonded. However, marriage in its normal sense is not necessary as there is no childbirth or family life. As for sex itself, he tells us that 'a new arrival on the astral plane is still filled with all the thoughts and bodily desires intact.' He warns that there are spiritual voyeurs in the first heaven. They hover close to earth and 'get a vicarious thrill out of wandering into a bedroom as an undetected witness to sexual intercourse'.

After death human beings are neither male nor female, but both combined

Meek also tells us that after death the basic duality of human sexuality is laid bare. Humans are neither male nor female, but both combined. Part of the progression towards the higher spiritual realms apparently involves the integration of both aspects of one's being. Indeed, he reports messages from people in the third or fourth heaven who claim that they have lived on earth as both male and female physical beings, and suggests that this is a necessary aspect of true progress.

Is there a God?

According to his automatic writings, one of the most surprising things that Monsignor Benson encountered during his early treks through heaven was 'a medium-sized building in the Gothic style and it resembled the parish church familiar on earth'.

But, he added, since there was no time as we know it in the afterlife, there was no list of times for services. When the minister decided to hold one 'whoever is in charge has only to send out his thoughts to his congregation and those that wish to come assemble forthwith.'

The idea of countless churches, apparently of all denominations, still teaching their individual messages to the faithful, even in heaven, seems bizarre. Monsignor Benson points out that it is a legacy of earth life, and we have to remember that the afterlife is created in the image of our world because of the mental states of those who pass over.

So where is God? Those who have died evidently retain their belief in a creator, but do not suddenly see someone sitting on a golden throne just because they have shuffled off this mortal coil. The gradual awareness of the higher levels within the afterlife leaves room for an aspiration to keep searching for God, but the expectation that one will find salvation simply as a matter of course following one's death is, according to all accounts, incorrect. Those in the second heaven seem no more aware of who or what God may be than you or I. They are forced to continue their spiritual quest.

How do we spend our time?

When we pass to the new world we still possess the same interests, levels of intelligence and prejudices that we had on earth. This means that our pursuits tend to follow similar lines. We are told that being in heaven is a little like retirement. We are free to develop ourselves to the full without the pressures of work (in the earthly sense), and gain spiritually from exploring and learning about things which will benefit our growth.

Monsignor Benson tells of attending a classical music concert along with countless others in a gigantic outdoor auditorium. Not only are the musicians perfecting their art for pleasure, but the great composers also have new works to perform. Moreover, the music is purer and more spiritually uplifting than anything on earth, and creates a glowing light show that rises from the auditorium and moves to blend with the music. From this we envisage a kind of laser light show, a concept undreamed of on earth when Benson's message was first conveyed.

This apparent foreknowledge of earth technology may be explained by the idea, conveyed by several sources, that scientists and inventors continue their life work in heaven. Their inspiration may then be 'beamed back' to earth. The way in which scientists such as Nick Muller aided Spiricom and even better-known dead souls such as Edison are supposedly assisting Vidicom illustrates this point.

Monsignor Benson tells of his visit to the 'Hall of Science' in a great afterlife city. Here all the best-known minds, now dead, were working on inventions decades ahead of laboratories on earth. This does make sense – if we can envisage the greatest scientists who ever lived having formed a heavenly cooperative and being unfettered by time and the problems of obtaining research grants. But it is perhaps odd that they all chose to work near where Benson lived.

In this venue Benson learned that 'in the past ages all the epoch-making discoveries have come from the spirit world. Of himself, incarnate man can do very little.' However, because of our abuse of what is given 'the earth world has not spiritually progressed enough to have many more splendid inventions than have already been perfected here. They are ready and waiting, but if they were sent through to the earth-plane in its present state of spiritual mind, they would be misused by unscrupulous people.'

This raises numerous intriguing possibilities. It is certainly true that discoveries on earth are often made by fascinating methods. The chemist Kekulé made the important discovery of the nature of a sub-atomic structure when he dreamed of a ring of snakes devouring each other's tails – the correct molecular shape. The planet Neptune was discovered by at least two people thousands of miles apart, but more or less concurrently as if in some kind of psychic link. After years of futile searching, their inspired guesswork on where to look appears to bear the hallmarks of outside influence.

Rather more difficult to understand is how, if this fine judgement is practised in heaven and discoveries are deliberately held back, someone 'up there' thought it a good idea to let through the secrets of the atomic bomb.

As Oliver Lodge noted, if scientists in the afterlife were able to intervene directly in the lives of people on earth: 'do you really think that the world would be in such a state as it is today?'

Questions like these seem hard to understand from this side, perhaps because that is the only side that we can see. Our earthly viewpoint may colour our judgement of the fundamental basis of knowledge and the very purpose of our existence. If you accept the possibility that nobody ever dies – and argue that they are 'promoted' and presumably work on from another sphere – then even the most tragic and inconceivable passing takes on new meaning. If there is a life after death, it will surely play a major part in answering the great questions that scientists and philosophers have tried in vain to answer for thousands of years.

MODERN SCIENCE, GOD AND THE AFTERLIFE

*I*s there any possible basis for accepting these fantastic-sounding stories? Could there really be trillions of dead people living in spirit houses on a plane of existence that links with our own? Surely science would dispute this?

Some scientists, of course, do reject these messages. Perhaps they are right to do so, for some information from heaven must simply be wrong. For instance, if some say heaven is on planet Marduk whilst others tell us that it is in a circle around the earth, at least one of them is wrong. On the other hand, some elements of these differing views of heaven interlock quite neatly. While sounding convincing is no substitute for reliable proof, it may not be a bad starting point.

Is there a conspiracy among scientists to prevent the results of Ron Pearson's work being heard?

Michael Roll has made a special study of the way scientists respond to the concept of the afterlife and has reached some astounding conclusions, as he told us at a conference in Cardiff. His work stems from first-hand research with theoretical scientist Ron Pearson, who, Roll says about this modest researcher from Bath, has proved survival beyond any possible doubt and will go down as the greatest scientist in history. Why, then, do so few people know of Pearson? Because, Roll believes, there is a conspiracy on the part of the scientific establishment to prevent the results of his work from being heard.

It is certainly true that in the early twentieth century science discovered a shocking reality that lay behind the seeming solidity of everyday life. All objects that we think of as real, from a table to an elephant, turn out to be just empty space filled by a whirling mass of energy that our eyes cannot grasp. We envisage a solid universe, yet it is anything but.

So close are the discoveries of modern science to much older beliefs about the afterlife that it has struck a number of researchers very forcibly. Perhaps the basis of reality as we now understand it (termed quantum mechanics) may establish these Spiritualist images as scientifically plausible. Great minds such as Albert Einstein, William Crookes (who actually became a spiritualist) and Sir Arthur Eddington – the very people who forged our modern understanding of the universe – spoke in terms that seem very mystical. They mentioned God and noted that the stuff of the universe is mind stuff; some saw the undeniable parallels between the inner world of sub-atomics and the mythic realms of the afterlife. Many pioneer modern physicists became closet believers in survival after death and felt that their work had gone some way towards establishing that possibility.

Ignorance of this fact is the conspiracy to which Michael Roll refers, although we feel it stems more from scientists' natural caution. Eighty years after Einstein set the course for the splitting of the atom, physics is still struggling to explain the staggering universe which has been unravelled. Physicists such as Dr Paul Davies at the University of Adelaide in Australia are able to write books which openly link God and science. He has even been awarded a grant of more than a million dollars, not from the usual sources that fund science but from a religious body which sees the importance of his ideas. Not so very long ago that kind of deal would have been impossible – perhaps even regarded as heresy. Today it shows that the gap between science and religion is narrowing, and soon we may have to accept that they are speaking the same language.

Great scientific minds such as Albert Einstein, William Crookes and Sir Arthur Eddington spoke in terms that seem very mystical

Chapter 11

HEAVEN SENT

VISIONS and other manifestations of those who have died – ghosts, for want of a better word – are reported in numerous different contexts. Over two-thirds of recently bereaved people, for instance, say that they feel the presence of their dead loved one in some way. It may simply be a sensation of being watched over, or it may consist of more concrete experiences in which familiar smells, sounds or images are detected around the house.

LIKE AN ELECTRIC LIGHT

DIANA Carter from Essex explains what happened to her in 1985 after the death of her fifty-six-year-old husband from a heart attack. Two months later she was telephoning her sister 'when all of a sudden I glanced at the stairs and my husband suddenly appeared as if an electric light was switched on. ... I yelled out. My sister asked what was wrong. I couldn't tell her at the time, so I just made up an excuse about reflections and cars going by. When I put the phone down my husband appeared down the stairs beside me about one yard away. I just stood looking at him. I wasn't in the least bit perturbed this time. Gradually the light which was surrounding him drew towards my left eye and disappeared.'

Over the next few weeks Diana saw her husband several times in dreams or visions. She said he looked younger and on one occasion he was staring out across a pink sky. Now she expects him to be waiting for her when it is her time to go.

A SENSE OF FAMILIARITY

PSYCHOLOGISTS argue that it is only an illusion. You have become so used to a particular person's presence, perhaps over many years, that until you adapt to their absence you feel as if they are still there.

An element of this may well be at work. But according to the countless communications being sent to us from heaven something more is going on. We are told that it is common for the spirit to stay near earth as if it still has a role to play in lives left behind. Many spirits even allegedly attend their own funeral service, if they are alert enough after recently arriving in the second heaven.

COMING TO TAKE YOU HOME

THERE is another time when the dead loved one may possibly return, even after many years in the afterlife. The dying say they are led into heaven by someone who was once close to them in life.

In August 1984 Jenny Randles was a patient in a Merseyside hospital. Also in her ward was a seventy-two-year-old cancer patient named Lucia. Lucia told Jenny that in 1971, only two days after her husband had died from cancer, he had appeared beside her bed at night to tell her how much he missed her. She was adamant that it had not been a dream. Now, as she fought with the same disease, she told Jenny that he had appeared again – this time in the hospital ward.

Lucia had got out of bed at three that morning to put on her dressing gown as she felt chilly. After she had clambered back a sudden stillness and silence seemed to fill the air and she noticed a curious distortion, as if time had lost all meaning. By the window was her husband, wearing a suit that he had loved in life. Lucia knew that he had come to take her to heaven, but she rebelled and said that she was not ready to go. He apparently smiled, and Lucia added that she would call him when *she* was ready – not before! With that he vanished. Lucia, still beaming with joy, repeated this story with total assurance.

A sudden stillness and silence seemed to fill the air and she noticed a curious distortation, as if time had lost all meaning

PSYCHIC VOYEURS

AMERICAN psychic Mabel Rowland warned that, whilst some post-death visitation such as this is quite normal, its continuation to the point of obsession may indicate a problem. Those who are too attached to material issues that have no place in the afterlife cling to earth just to get their fix. 'There are hordes of these pitiful earthbound souls,' she tells us, 'haunting clearing houses, counting houses, money markets and trade centres of all sorts.' She also suggests that a few spirits may haunt bars and pubs.

Nevertheless the usual motive for return visits appears to be to advise relatives of one's continued existence. That is a common urge soon after passing over and it forms the usual basis for messages conveyed by mediums. It is as if the person in the afterlife scans around to find a person on their wavelength and hopes that they can get word across to some relative. This is how so called 'drop-in' communications occur, from people who are unknown to the medium.

'I can still see him although he doesn't know it... I wanted him to have something from me'

That task may sound difficult but it is not necessarily so. For example, comedienne Marti Caine, who died from cancer in November 1995, was back in touch within days through Lincolnshire medium Helen Christian. They had never known one another in life. According to the Spiritualist, as she sat at her computer she had a vision of the performer and rapidly typed up what she was told. Reputedly, Marti asked Helen, 'Tell everyone I'm fine' and added that 'Gran is here looking after me'. She went on, with a smile, 'My hat's on straight' and said with a chuckle, 'Life is a doddle up here.' More significantly, she offered a personal message for 'my soul mate' – whom she named – and asked the startled medium, to whom this all meant little, to report to him that, 'I can still see him, although he doesn't know it . . . . He was great to me in the end. Such a tough time. I'm sad about him. I wanted him to have something from me. That is why I asked this lady to help.'

Such innocence almost begs one to believe in it – although, of course, the newspapers at the time were full of stories about Marti Caine's life and death and few people could have been unaware of them. More typically, the drop-in is someone whose death has provoked no national headlines.

SUMS GREATER THAN THEIR PARTS

How can we be sure that a communication received via a medium is genuine? Something special seems to be required to establish that such messages actually come from outside the sitter's mind. The classic cross-correspondences are the prime example and have never been surpassed – nor, sadly, have they ever really been equalled. For thirty years, from 1901 onwards, a vast series of messages, seeming to originate from classical scholar F. W. Myers after his death, were received by mediums who were often thousands of miles apart. Each picked up a message that meant little on its own but formed part of a very complex jigsaw. When all the pieces of the puzzle were slotted together it was seen to contain literary allusions that seemed to reflect a rational, intelligent mind.

Something similar occurred in the 1930s when Spiritualist Maurice Barnabell founded the movement's weekly newspaper, *Psychic News*. On the day that his accountant first suggested the idea to him he attended a seance at which medium Estelle Roberts told him of a message from the afterlife: it was urging him to give up his other pursuits and concentrate on spreading the news about Spiritualism. Later, Barnabell appeared in secret at a sitting with medium Kathleen Barkel. She reported that Lord Northcliffe, the famous dead newspaper baron, had come to the seance. When asked why, it was reported that their new (unidentified) sitter had plans to launch a Spiritualist newspaper and that Northcliffe wanted to be there to give his support. The next time Barnabell returned to sit with Estelle Roberts he was asked by her guide if he was finally convinced to act now that he had had the message during the other seance, although he had told nobody about it. Were those in the afterlife aware of what another was saying via different mediums?

Lord Northcliffe said he had come to the seance to give support from the afterlife to the new Spiritualist newspaper

GHOSTS

In the popular imagination ghosts are usually perceived as terrifying apparitions – semi-ethereal forms that moan and wail. Nothing could be further from the truth. Whether ghosts are a reality or some form of hallucination, they appear as ordinary human beings and are often impossible to distinguish from someone who is alive.

We'll meet again

Alan Bell wrote to us to describe his experience, which began with the tragic death of his sister at the age of five. Because of a family row, some of his father's relatives did not attend the funeral. As a result, when Andrew's paternal grandmother later died he in turn refused to go to that funeral because he could not forgive the way her side of the family had let an innocent child become the victim of a petty dispute.

Soon afterwards, feeling guilty, Andrew had a vivid dream in which he saw his grandmother. He seized this opportunity to apologise to her for not attending the funeral, and she told him that he was forgiven. Despite the realism of this dream, Andrew understandably points out that it could have been his guilty conscience at work, attempting to assuage his feelings by conjuring up a hallucination.

However, the same argument is more difficult to apply to the experience of his six-year-old brother who returned from school to announce that he had been playing with his dead sister. There was not a trace of fear or surprise on his face as he described this event. To him it was quite natural that she had 'gone somewhere else' but could return for a brief meeting.

As Andrew notes, with adults there are complicated motives to take into account. With children, things are usually a good deal more straightforward; when they say they have seen a ghost, and are still too young to know that such an event is 'impossible', perhaps we should listen.

He became aware of a presence standing over him, which was human-like but not human

To fight another day

Perhaps the most astonishing tale of a post-mortal vision comes from a former American soldier who we shall call Felix. One night in 1966, during the Vietnam War, he was at a firebase camp. In the early hours he suddenly became aware of a presence standing over him. He knew it was human-like – but not human. It exuded the feeling that it was a ghost. Felix lay face down on the ground with his eyes closed; he was desperate to move, but remained motionless in accordance with training. He was well aware that any sudden movement could give his position away to the enemy or even scare a trigger-happy guard on his own side who would shoot before establishing whether he was friend or foe.

There was no problem until the apparition touched him. So shocked was Felix by this act that all his training went out of the window and he leaped into the air, passing right through the space where the figure had been standing. That space was empty. Felix crashed into a trench a few feet away, landing on top of another soldier who was rudely awoken by the impact and fearing that he was under attack by the Viet Cong, started to fight.

OPPOSITE PAGE *A genuine ghost? This photograph was taken at Raynham Hall in Norfolk and shows a figure known as the 'Brown Lady'*

The struggle lasted only seconds before it was interrupted by a whistling sound as a mortar shell roared through the air and struck the ground where Felix had just been lying. It was the only shell to strike their camp that night and must have been launched from too great a distance for Felix to have been heard by the enemy. The men were thrown into chaos by the snap raid, but when the tension subsided one question nagged at them. How had Felix known this shell was coming well before it could have been heard? He told them the truth – a ghost had saved his life.

Trapped on earth

According to researchers, ghosts are not always earthbound for beneficial reasons. Indeed, they argue that visitors from the first heaven or lower astral planes can become a real nuisance. This may not necessarily be the fault of the spirit itself. A case in point involves a poltergeist – a noisy, mischievous spirit – that attacked a house in Doncaster in 1992. Angela Blake had been driven to despair by the events that plagued her home. Doors would open on their own, water taps would switch on and off and the cooker kept lighting itself without human intervention. In the end, medium Sandy Thompson offered to check things out.

At the house, Sandy claimed to establish contact with the spirit of a dead man. The information she gave included his name, Frank Warburton, and the fact that he had been a diabetic. This stunned Angela Blake for she recognised the name: Frank Warburton had lived in the house many years earlier. It was eventually decided that Frank, though dead, was still 'living' in the house, and the only solution was to try to get him to move out. Sandy and another medium joined forces and contacted the spirit. Frank took over Sandy's vocal cords and began to speak through her mouth.

> *The poltergeist had difficulty opening doors in the house, so it drew energy from the family's youngest child*

A story emerged which suggested that Frank the poltergeist was unaware that he was no longer alive. Because he could still see the house he tried to live in it, but had difficulty in opening doors. To make this possible, he had to draw energy from the Blakes' youngest child. He also seemed to want to stay on earth because of a family row and a desperate desire to contact his living daughter. Eventually the daughter was found and a reconciliation began, but, according to Sandy Thompson, Frank could only be persuaded to move from the lower astral planes into the second heaven when his mother's spirit was asked to descend from there and urge him to join her.

Fascinating as all this is, it begs a question or two. Why was Frank's mother not waiting for him at the point of his death – as in so many other alleged cases – and why did she need to be asked before she came to rescue her son?

PHYSICAL MEDIUMSHIP

CLAIMS by psychics that they can communicate with spirits in the afterlife are all very well – but if you yourself are not able to 'tune in' to these messages or see the visions they see, you will always have to take their word for it. But there is one extraordinary type of mediumship in which that is not the case. Physical mediums can allegedly bring the dead back for everyone to witness.

This supposedly happens through ectoplasm extracted from the etheric body of the medium (see p. 121). During a materialisation seance the dead communicator reputedly puts on this substance like an overcoat in order to appear physically in the room. In this way a seemingly living version of the discarnate spirit is witnessed by everyone present, and can be touched and photographed.

In the early days of Spiritualism, when materialisation mediums were common, this kind of seance was often the subject of trickery. Mediums usually sat in cabinets out of sight, and only much later was it discovered that when the lights went out many of them would move about in the dark pretending to be the returning spirits. Muslin and other soft, gauze-like materials were used to create the ghostly look or to represent ecto-plasm. Countless dubious spirit photographs were produced in this way. Were *any* of the physical mediums genuine?

The evidence of Noah's Ark

The oddly named Noah's Ark Society has been set up to promote this rare kind of mediumship in today's world in the hope that it will prove the existence of life after death beyond any shadow of a doubt. In such cases there can be no middle ground. Either a cruel hoax is involved, or the dead really do return.

One of the leaders of the Noah's Ark team, George Cranley, believes that we already possess some very strong evidence. He cites cases in which, during a seance, physical mediums have produced countless three-dimensional manifestations which have lasted long enough to be examined by doctors present in the room. Dr Douglas Baker, commenting on a session with medium Alec Harris, reports how during the experiments a wide range of individuals appeared. They included men, young women, old women and even babies. He was able to use a stethoscope to test their breathing and feel their pulse. Baker says of one: 'I noted carefully the warmth of the flesh, the firmness of the limbs. The pulse beat seemed normal. Veins, hard prominences, etc., all appeared to be present as with a normal human.'

It is hard to imagine a ghost with a pulse or varicose veins

It is hard to imagine a ghost with a pulse or varicose veins. To the doctor, and to George Cranley, this testing vindicates materialisation mediumship as proof of survival. Others might feel that the very human nature of the returning spirits implies that human is exactly what they were. However, nobody can deny the integrity and ideals of the Noah's Ark team.

Is it genuine?

Why has materialisation mediumship waned so dramatically? Cynics might well point out that it coincided with the rise in the testing of Spiritualism and the exposure of so many frauds. It may also not be irrelevant that infra-red and low-light photography now make it possible to film in the dark, thus ensuring that once-simple trickery is now easy to expose.

Those who study the phenomenon point out that darkness is essential to protect the medium, because the loss of ectoplasm during the seance is stressful, even life-threatening. They cite the case of Helen Duncan, one of the last great physical mediums. She was harassed by the police during the 1940s and 1950s and even charged under the Witchcraft Act

– the last British person to suffer that fate. It is widely believed that her death in 1956 was the result of a police raid during a physical mediumship seance which she was forced to abandon in great haste. Certainly after the seance her health deteriorated and she died a few weeks later.

Thanks to the efforts of the Noah's Ark team there has been a small resurgence of materialisation mediumship, but the group are understandably very protective of the mediums with whom they work. Only small seances are set up, cameras are usually banned and the medium

Physical medium Helen Duncan producing ectoplasm during a seance. She was the last person to be charged under the British Witchcraft Act

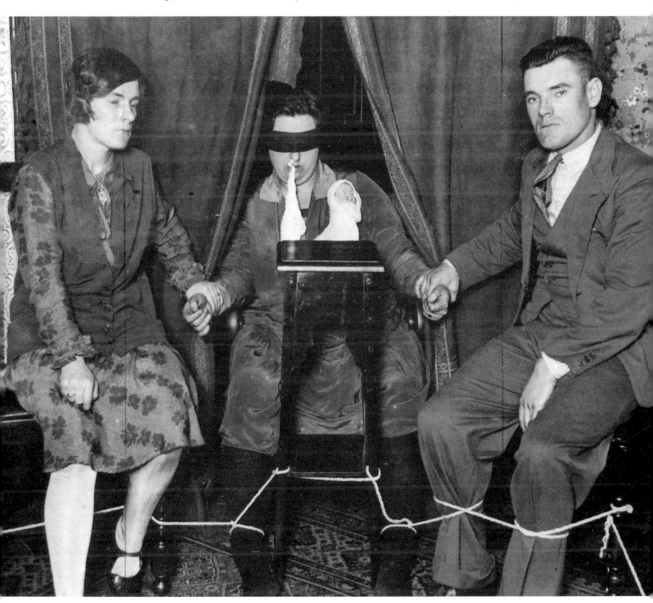

works in darkness and may not be touched. The medium is also often tied to a chair and left out of sight in a cabinet, something which many sceptics find difficult to understand.

A mini-scandal erupted in 1992 when an investigator sneaked a camera into a seance. The lights were switched on and various physical phenomena, for instance a trumpet supposedly moving through the room on its own, were now seen to be produced by the medium himself, who was holding the trumpet in his hands! The person who revealed this fraud was banned from future sessions because of his 'deception' in using the camera without permission. It was decided that the medium had been possessed by an evil force during this particular seance. His own spirit guide had switched on the lights to show up the infesting entity and thus free the medium, who continues to be highly regarded within Spiritualist circles.

Some people may find it rather convenient that at the one seance at which photographs were taken hoaxing was found to be at work, albeit allegedly as a result of psychic factors. Are we really to believe that all other experiments with physical mediums around the world involve genuine materialisations, even if this one did not? We have no way of knowing the truth, of course, but caution seems an appropriate response.

'Hello, Mum. It's your son, Alan,' said the young man who had been murdered fourteen years earlier

The other side of the story comes from a Basildon woman who claims that perhaps today's best-respected physical medium, Lincoln, produced her dead son for her in late 1994. The youth had been murdered in 1980 but reputedly appeared and walked across the room to greet her with the words: 'Hello, Mum. It's your son, Alan.'

Over the next few minutes the woman had a long conversation with her son and was able to touch him. She says that he felt completely normal and was warm-blooded. His hands were even rough, as she would expect, given that he had worked in the building trade.

As with other materialisation mediumship cases this event occurred in the dark, so any physical resemblance between the spirit and Mrs Brown's son cannot easily be ascertained. But there is no doubt that this particular mother was convinced that her son lived on and had paid a return visit from heaven.

George Cranley is sure that this kind of evidence will be further improved. He says that scientists in the spirit world are attempting to push forward the methods that allow physical mediumship. It is supposedly their decision that so little has been seen in recent years because, after the death of Helen Duncan, they decided to protect mediums until they could find a way to avoid the risks. Soon they will supposedly allow a red light, such as those used in a photographic darkroom, to operate during the experiments, and this might permit some photography.

Meantime Michael Roll is trying to persuade the Noah's Ark Society to allow him to set up tests using low-light cameras, but worries over the danger to the medium have so far prevented them from agreeing. But perhaps one day soon this kind of evidence will silence the doubts that are otherwise bound to persist.

Chapter 12

TIMELESSNESS AND THE OZ FACTOR

THE OZ factor is the name given to a particular state of consciousness which is very similar to the kind of timelessness said to be found in the afterlife. The stories of NDEs, alien abductions and assorted visions in this chapter may appear to be a random selection, but they all demonstrate the Oz Factor and may be part of a continuum that tells us much about reality in the allegedly mind-created universe.

Caroline from Zimbabwe describes it well. Immediately prior to the onset of her experience with a bright light, then meeting strange mystical beings, and finally being spacenapped, she says: 'Everything was silent. Even the crickets had stopped chirping, I felt cut off from everybody.'

A teenager from Bangor, Northern Ireland, was about to become engulfed by 'the purest white light I have ever seen'. This is a term that NDE victims often allude to, of course. He says that suddenly all the noise on the busy road outside his house disappeared. It was as if only he and this wonderful phenomenon existed, locked together in time and space. Time spread out 'like strawberry jam'.

Bobby, a young boy who stood as if paralysed while a truck bore down on him in North Carolina, USA, was rescued by what we might variously term a miracle, angelic intervention or an alien presence. More importantly, this experience was marked by the onset of a strange feeling which included the disappearance of background noise, the linking together of Bobby with this phenomenon on an intimate level and the sense that time had lost all meaning. No longer could Bobby measure it as we normally do. For the 'eternity' of this experience it was as if there was no time at all. Indeed, perhaps time, as experienced during these various phenomena, provides the key to our understanding of an after-life experience.

ALL THE TIME IN THE WORLD

IN claims about life after death, why is it that some children who die very young grow up suddenly, whilst others are still children when they return to their families during seances many years later? If time is more difficult, or impossible, to gauge in an afterlife without clocks or body rhythms, how can its residents keep track of the passing years back on earth?

This presents a difficulty, because many communications from heaven stress the timeless nature of their senders' new existence. But if there is no time how can one be aware of existence, which surely depends upon judging how we progress from moment to moment?

As we are so constrained to think in terms of clock measurements on earth we cannot conceive of a timeless reality – it may simply be beyond our comprehension to do so. Yet we are forced into that predicament when we imagine the universe because it appears to be timeless, eternal and infinite.

Many messages stress that in heaven there is only eternity, and this forces an entirely different perspective on things. Time is a human invention to take account of the changing seasons and other cycles in our mundane reality. But at a spiritual level such things are unnecessary and time does not exist. Where no time is needed, many things are possible that seem to us like magic.

Time is a human invention to take account of the changing seasons and other cycles in our mundane reality

THE DEADWOOD SAGE

DORSET medium Sandy Bullock started to get messages from a most unexpected source – his namesake (and possible distant relative) Seth Bullock. Seth claimed to be the sheriff of the town of Deadwood, South Dakota, over a hundred years ago. The medium says he had never heard of him or the town – although Doris Day's song 'The Deadwood Stage' from the film *Calamity Jane* readily springs to mind.

Contact with the present sheriff confirmed that Seth Bullock had indeed been in charge in 1876. Moreover, ghostly goings-on had afflicted his old house, now converted into a hotel.

Sheriff Bullock, determined to prove his survival, passed on much information through the English medium and was able to answer very specific questions about his life and the condition of the town today – which would probably be impossible for someone who has never visited the spot. The deceased Bullock also claimed to be able to see into the future from his timeless position in the afterlife, warning of a new 'Gold Rush' that would strike the town and create trouble for the present lawmen. This seemed absurb until it was revealed that Deadwood was introducing new gambling laws and problems were occurring due to the influx of strangers in pursuit of 'gold'.

Deadwood, South Dakota, USA in 1876. Dorset medium Sandy Bullock says that he has received messages from one Seth Bullock, a sheriff of Deadwood over a hundred years ago

Deadwood in 1876

LOST MEMORY

IN November 1980 a West Yorkshire police officer named Alan Godfrey claimed to have had a close encounter with a UFO in the town of Todmorden. At five o'clock on a cold morning he lost all memory of about fifteen minutes of time. Eight months later he was hypnotically regressed and recalled being abducted into a strange room where he met beings who seemed fascinated by his life.

The interpretation of this incident as a UFO abduction may only be a matter of semantics. In his memory Alan saw a great light, found himself floating out of the body and was then in a bright place in the presence of a wise being who communicated by some psychic means. It is easy to see why in the space age it would be tempting to call this an example of spacenapping by weird aliens, but we need only make a slight change in emphasis to reveal something very similar to a near death experience or even some kind of visionary spiritualist encounter with the afterlife realm.

INNER OR OUTER SPACE?

A woman called Jenny from Kent had a series of ghostly encounters when young and then one night, after stabling her horse, entered into what she described as a sort of spiritual communion with a glowing light. Her dog looked up at it, so it was real, not imaginary. She felt a direct mind-to-mind contact with a fantastic intelligence-draining emotion from her.

> 'I used to really look forward to going to bed as I had some playmates... beautiful lights'

Once again her case was considered to be an alien contact but it might just as well be termed a mystical or near death vision. As a child she recalls how 'strange balls of light came into my bedroom to play. I would call my mother to see them but they always disappeared before she got there.' These balls of light are a frequently reported feature of such encounters. Marie from Nottingham, who also experienced a spacenapping said that between the ages of four and eight 'I used to really look forward to going to bed as I had some playmates. These play-mates were beautiful lights.'

Shelley from Lancashire told of her series of childhood encounters which included the remarkable claim that she could float about her house. This sounds as if it were a vivid form of out-of-body experience. It eventually led to an alien abduction during which the strange beings she met behind the white light told her that she had an important task to perform, but that her conscious mind was not to know what it was. Only when 'the sequence of events' unfolded would it become clear. This is another common theme – that of wise beings in control of our time and space, using those whom they contact as channels.

Sent back to the pain of his physical self, he was warned that 'demons' would be encountered as he neared earth again

---

What do we make of the man who almost died in a Middlesbrough dentist surgery after reacting badly to the anaesthetic? He found himself floating free of his body and drifting up through the ceiling into a place where he met what he thought were aliens. They sent him back to the pain of his physical self, but warned that 'demons' would be encountered as he neared earth on his way home and they would be keen to 'possess' his body. He would have to fight them off, which he did, returning as the dentist thumped his chest and desperately tried to bring him round.

This took place in 1964 and was reported to us as an alien contact. More obviously it is an example of a near death vision with many of the classic features. Note also how descent through the lower astral planes – as recounted in 'postcards from heaven' – fits very neatly with the idea of this man encountering demons who prey on vulnerable spirits and seek to possess their bodies.

This case, which seems to be a blend between near death and abduc-tion, is by no means unique. There are many other examples of reports that could be either NDEs or spacenappings, and even the leading near-death researcher, Dr Kenneth Ring has taken note of them in his work at the University of Connecticut. But nobody has quite figured out what these unexpected parallels mean.

Perhaps there is a clue in the fact that famous Spiritualist mediums such as Betty Shine and Doris Collins also claim to have had alien contact experiences during their lifetime of spiritual encounters. These occurred in the same way as their telepathic visions of the afterlife, but the mediums believe that this time they were in touch with non-earthly life forms.

Possibly all of these things are more intimately related than we realise. Indeed, maybe the differences are more to do with our

Famous medium Betty Shine claims to have had alien contact experiences during her lifetime of spiritual encounters

evaluation of the experience than with its cosmic realities. Either way, the real key could be that these are all happening at the level of an altered state of consciousness where time and space are not as we know it. This 'true' reality may be the closest that we can get (this side of heaven) to what it is like to exist without a body.

MINDSCAPE

PERHAPS the problem is that we try to evaluate the ineffable through our rational mind, so inevitably we place false interpretations on what we see. But the truth behind these many strange experiences can only be grasped intuitively and through that inner, spiritual awareness that we can only touch through altered states of consciousness – those timeless states that are precipitated by the Oz Factor.

In the *Tibetan Book of the Dead* the post-death world is purely image-based and time-independent. It tells of events that span years or decades but which seem to be instantaneous. It reports how we wander through a mindscape of thought-created experiences: 'As men think so are they, both here and hereafter, thoughts being things, the parents of all actions.'

*'Everything is inter-related.
Reality is, after all, a state of
mind, of consciousness'*

Gilbert Bonner, a psychotherapist and one of the leading experts in the field of electronic communications with the afterlife, seems aware of this problem. 'I believe reality and imagination can flow into each other,' he says. 'Everything is inter-related. Reality is, after all, a state of mind, of consciousness.' He is echoing the discoveries of modern physics, which prove that the mind is the architect of all that we see – not simply a camera that records what is there (see p. 132). Of course, if we can do this in the material plane there is no reason to dismiss the Spiritualist view of an afterlife produced by a vast collective unconscious forged from everyone who has died. Indeed, we would expect to encounter this because it is much what we seem to have on earth. We just do not accept on a day-to-day level what science is telling us – that the solidity of our world is in truth a ghostly phantasm which our mind has created for us out of brain wave patterns and fluctuating quantum energies.

American psychologist William James, a specialist in altered states, noted that our normal waking consciousness (what we think of as 'reality') was but one state, separated by the 'filmiest of screens' from many other states which were always present. We could visit them in dreams, or by using stimulants such as drugs. Some, who were psychically aware, could go there more readily.

Perhaps most of us see little of these things until that moment when we cross over into the after-death state.

Chapter 13

THE SECOND DEATH

TWO themes emerge from the gradual progression up the hierarchy of heaven. They both involve what is sometimes referred to as 'the second death' because it concerns a complete change of environment and a drastic departure from the idyllic pleasures of the afterlife.

This change may be a move into the rarified levels of the upper heavens, where materialism is all but absent and one is wrenched from familiar things – it is easy to understand the analogy with death. On the other hand the second death may involve travel downwards to return to the leaden shackles of the earth plane. That means, of course, that one is reborn – reincarnated as a different human being.

The experiences of those in our own world who believe they have lived a previous existence were described in Chapter 5. This chapter discusses the views of mediums and those who have already passed into the afterlife.

ONE LIFE ONLY?

THE idea of reincarnation is one of the most contentious within Spiritualism. It is either accepted or rejected, and there is no obvious consensus. What is worse, the messages from guides are very often contradictory.

Robert Benson does not discuss the matter, but from the context of his account of life in the second heaven it is obvious that reincarnation never enters the equation. He refers to spirits who are centuries old living on at higher levels, and there is an old-fashioned lack of sexual equality in much of what he says. At one point he even refers to a fellow soul, Ruth, with the rather patronising attitude that there were lots of things a woman could do in heaven.

More importantly, this whole concept of male and female is further proof that in Monsignor Benson's heaven there is no place for reincarnation. For the whole essence of past lives is that the soul is essentially androgynous and can incarnate many times as either male or female. Although it would seem difficult to imagine the afterlife being populated by people whose image of themselves is different from their most recent life (meaning that they are viewed as being either male or female) Benson clearly has something more fundamental in mind. To him what we were in life is what we are.

Again, to him eternity seems to go in only one direction – from conception via life into death and ever onward in this timeless heaven. Prior to our birth on earth, there seems to have been no place for us at all in this cosmic scheme of things. The disquieting outcome is the impression of new souls being created by the truckload every few minutes and sent to earth to be born. This must create a population explosion in heaven, as new deaths are forever escalating the numbers who arrive at a rate which must tax eternity itself.

Of course, Benson lived in an era when reincarnation had not been accepted by Western culture to any degree (he died in 1914). This is, after all, a relatively recent phenomenon in the West, beginning in the mid-fifties and only gaining foothold in the sixties and seventies. The suspicion arising is, sadly, that Monsignor Benson's heaven is a little too customised. It suited the beliefs of the era from which it emerged, but is less appropriate to the changing perspective of the 1990s.

The problem is this. If there is an actual afterlife to which universal laws apply, and if Borgia's automatic writings were genuine postcards sent to us from that heaven, it should have reflected absolute truth, not the truth as the society of his day would have preferred.

The soul is essentially androgynous and can incarnate many times as either male or female

THE BEGINNINGS OF A SPIRITUAL REVOLUTION

EVEN today the battle lines are drawn: views about life in heaven continue to reflect the intense dispute over reincarnation. Medium Doris Collins gave us her opinion, based on more than seventy years of

Anthony Borgia who channelled Monsignor Robert Benson through automatic writing

'We have broken away from the great supreme source of life and...when we are perfected enough... we will be embraced back'

receiving messages from the afterlife. 'We have broken away from the great supreme source of life and at some stage – when we are perfected enough – we will be embraced back. I am a great believer now in reincarnation. I did not always believe in it. But because of certain [messages] – which were quite provable – I do believe it. I think I have lived before. I think I have used my gift before. I think that certain child prodigies who are so knowledgeable have also used their gift before.'

But how does anyone make a difference in this world if all memory of our previous lives and afterlives are eliminated by rebirth? The usual response, from all great philosophies on reincarnation as well as post-cards from heaven, is that at the level of the spirit we do not forget.

Many guides claim that the 'matter world' makes us want to forget: There are too many distractions and we become lazy about spiritual matters. But things are not as gloomy as they sound. We have made substantial progress during the past century or so. Comparing civilisation in many parts of the world with just a short time ago we see greater social justice such as no penal servitude for trivial indiscretions, more recognition of the fundamental philosophies behind the dogma of religious beliefs, and some true revolutions such as the banishing of slavery. This is said to be the result of souls reincarnating at an ever more prodigious rate and injecting some spiritual awareness into the planet.

The two world wars of the twentieth century have killed millions, but those souls have often returned after unusually short periods in heaven. They have a much greater opportunity to put things right on earth because their own prior sufferings have given them a huge incentive to ensure that these terrible events are never repeated.

Medium Bill Tenuto, passing on the words of the White Brotherhood (a collection of souls in the afterlife who try to make changes on the earth plane), tells us that a great spiritual revolution is underway. The increased levels of interest in the paranormal and the millions who are now seeking a path toward enlightenment respond to this concerted inspiration. It is all part of a cosmic plan.

*O*H YES IT IS – OH NO IT ISN'T!

NOTED materialisation medium Lincoln faced a huge London audience in 1994 as part of a Spiritualist festival. He entered a trance and had offered to allow his spirit guide, a Victorian publishing baron known as Magnus, to answer any questions about life after death. When specifically challenged about reincarnation, in the form of a question that clearly assumed that Magnus would support its existence, the reply was unexpectedly dramatic.

'I hoped this question would not arise,' Magnus bemoaned. 'You will have but one physical life. If you experience within yourself memories of a previous existence this is not from you personally but from the memories of those attachments who are with you.' He asked the audience to consider that 'if the human spirit is designed for progression, what would be the purpose of continually returning to earth? This, I would say, is regression.'

'If the human spirit is designed for progression, what would be the purpose of continually returning to earth?'

Roy Stemman, editor of *Reincarnation International*, hit out at this in the pages of *Psychic News*, appealing to Spiritualists not to 'base your beliefs on the words of one spirit guide'. He points out that other highly respected guides have pronounced in favour of rebirth, also that Magnus himself professes not to be all-knowing. However, one might expect such a fundamental principle of the universe not to be at issue in the afterlife. Otherwise, where do the post-mortal inhabitants think that all these souls suddenly go for three score years and ten?

Stemman rightly ponders that the blatant discrepancies between the messages from these guides on such important issues leaves one wondering who to believe. Indeed, they appear rather similar to the differences between major religions on vital doctrine. The problem is that these religious views are philosophies forged on earth, whereas the spirit guides are supposedly speaking from first-hand experience of heaven and therefore ought to be more consistent.

The differences of opinion also settle on issues such as the precise moment when a soul incarnates. Lincoln – who, remember, is talking of the one and only birth that he says we have – alleges that this occurs at the point of conception. Some evidence of claimed memories of people who say they recall life in the womb might support this view. But other guides vehemently disagree.

Their opinion is matched by an experience described by Russian medium Alexandra Yakovleva, who describes a mystical vision during the birth of her child at a Moscow hospital. 'I saw a human soul descending to earth. It was not unlike the visions described by people who have been in a state of clinical death – only in reverse.' She reports how entities in the afterlife were in conversation guiding the soul towards its destination and seeing the continent, country, city and hospital selected. Then 'I saw myself and a tiny baby lying by my side and I realised that this soul would be my child and I would be its mother. Then I came to.' If her vision is correct, this soul did not arrive at conception but nine months later.

THE 'TOTAL SOUL'

THE complexity of the issue is further expanded by a message reputedly conveyed by Raynor Johnson, a Spiritualist teacher who returned in 1993 (some six years after his death) via a Devon medium. He explained that his recent incarnation as a teacher owed something to a previous life during the infamous Inquisition, when he spread untruths to many people.

Johnson adds. 'I was a member of a group soul. Or, I should say, I am a member of a group soul.' This concept is a popular belief that souls share incarnation after incarnation as part of a team of individuals who interact and try to bring about necessary progress. They are consciously unaware of this link most of the time; although the expression 'soul mates', often used by people who feel they are on the same wavelength with another human being, is said to convey an inner recognition of these past life bonds.

Gateway was published in 1979 by Roger Whitby. The most unusual thing about it is that Whitby had died, aged twenty-two, sixteen years before he wrote this book. It was conveyed through a medium and church minister who happened to be his mother. In a vivacious and entertaining account of his present life in heaven, Whitby insists that reincarnation is real. But there is a twist. 'The total soul is ever-evolving. It is also free and can choose the point of incarnation. ... To know the whole when incarnate would be too much even if it were possible. It is not possible here until far advanced.'

Only part of the 'total soul' incarnates on earth - the rest stays in the afterlife and attempts to communicate with its earthly counterpart

---

Whitby further supports the idea of group souls incarnating together and says of these: 'We all learn differently and take from each other what we can best assimilate.' Stranger still, he tells us that only part of what he calls the 'total soul' incarnates on earth at one time. The rest of 'us' stays in the afterlife and attempts to communicate with its earthly counterpart – for instance during deep sleep. After death the two aspects of the soul must then reintegrate.

This curious claim may help to explain some of the difficulties regarding the sexless nature of the soul. For, as Whitby says, 'developing, evolving consciousness is sexless. Quite seriously this is the eternal plan. ... It's all such a baffling, exciting and stupendous experience – this evolvement of conscious being. You forget so much of yourself – or of the self that seems so important lower down. You're caught up in such wonder, such a vibrating, pulsating spiral. I really can't describe it.'

THE WALL OF FIRE

BUT what of those who go through the second death and enter the higher levels of heaven? What is it like to experience this process? ·

It seems to be a shedding of all material attributes and an absorption into a fully mental state. Whilst to our way of thinking this might contribute a diminution of self, it is reputedly looked forward to as infinitely joyful. The act – just like death in this world – can be harrowing to contemplate for some, but it is not painful to endure – much as the transition from the earth plane to heaven is said to be far less traumatic in reality than it is in preconception.

In one of his messages Oliver Lodge justifies why this transformation is necessary. 'It would seem that at whatever level we find ourselves we reach the stage of a brick wall. No more progress can be made unless we have certain experiences.' Sometimes, he adds, this was to be found back on earth. But the second death and entry into the more spiritual realms of heaven could also be perceived as an opportunity for growth. Evolution was what it was all about.

Dr Joseph Kahn, a dead scientist speaking through the mediumship of Stephen Rudoff, spoke of the barrier that exists and which separates the familiar heaven from this place beyond our comprehension. It is not like the tunnel, the bright light and the invisible barrier that separates earthly life from the first stages of death; at least according to those who have near death experiences. This, says Kahn, is 'a wall of fire where matter ceases to exist'. It is perhaps one of the most awesome and unexpected images of life in heaven.

CONCLUSION: TO BELIEVE OR NOT

I N THIS book we have considered all sorts of evidence that there is survival after death. Some of it, such as the Spiricom and Vidicom messages, is in a form that anyone can judge. These are either a cruel hoax by someone somewhere, or are direct proof of an afterlife. Much more often, however, the evidence is anecdotal. We can, of course, invent explanations – such as wishful thinking, imagination or hallucinations. It is easy to dismiss such things as unimportant. But they are very important to the people to whom these experiences occur.

Performer and a former intelligence officer during World War Two, the late Michael Bentine, was also a gifted psychic. He told us of many messages that he has received which on occasion appear to have come from the afterlife. He also had a vision of the attempt to rescue the American hostages in Iran in 1980 before that event actually happened. Bentine told us that following his many personal experiences he has no doubt that we survive death. Nor did he find it difficult to accept this from a scientific perspective. 'It is very simple. You cannot destroy energy. It's a scientific fact. There is nothing complex about that.'

The late Michael Bentine was also a gifted psychic

This surety apart, science appears hopelessly out of touch with the wider and more spiritual issues that become progressively more important the older one gets. It flounders in the face of questions such as survival after death.

Not that involvement in this weird world of the supernatural should convince you of everything. Far from it. Much of the evidence comes down to mistaken identity. Wishful thinking dominates many case histories. Even the most extraordinary event can be open to several less dramatic interpretations if you are willing to probe deeply enough.

Messages from a medium may prove that there is a life beyond death. But there are other possibilities that always have to be excluded first. Some mediums are frauds – not necessarily conscious frauds. Often they practise the reading of body language and are adept at psychology. Mediums can be intuitive and pick up signals from their own subconscious mind which they wrongly interpret as coming from outside themselves as a message from a spirit in the afterlife. This need not always be (indeed sceptics would say it is never) the case. They make their skills fit their own belief systems in the same way that some scientists reject all things supernatural because they are not spoken of in their philosophy.

Truly gifted mediums seem to be rare, perhaps rarer than Spiritualism will admit. But there are cases where it seems reasonable to conclude that in certain circumstances we can gain access to information by way of powers beyond what is normal. Is that the same thing as stating that gifted mediums are in contact with heaven? Sadly not. If any paranormal power is at work it may well be ESP, or a sort of telepathy. Michael Bentine, as he himself recognised, could have 'tuned in' to a worried officer on the aircraft carrier in the Gulf contemplating the daring plan to rescue the hostages. His communication need not have come from heaven.

The dead have no voices but reputedly do have minds, so this is surely how any hypothetical contact between themselves and earth must take place. Unfortunately, it is also precisely how a medium would tune into the mind of someone who is still living. If people visit a medium it is inevitable that the visitors will be filling their minds with images of dead loved ones whom they hope might come through. Should a truly gifted medium then use ESP to pick up such an image, they may assume that it is from the deceased on a day trip from the afterlife – but how can they really know? Is it not just as likely that it is a vision plucked straight from the mind of the living sitter?

This is the real problem about the afterlife: so much of it rests upon mental communication, either through a medium or coming spontaneously via the mind of a witness. We have come across many cases where a medium seemed to be fishing through a sea of thoughts and plucking out a range of images, thus mixing up two or three sitters in their contact.

Another problem we have found is that in heaven bodily distortions are supposed to disappear. So why don't the mediums describe the deceased as they must be 'now' in heaven, if that is what they are really tuning in to? Instead, they often see dead people as others once knew them in life.

However, there are definite occasions when information could not come by this most obvious route – for example, news that the sitter did not know. These are very exciting to any cautious researcher. But even here we are not entirely safe because the phenomenon of cryptomnesia rears its head: perhaps you did know this fact and have simply forgotten about it. Unfortunately, spirits rarely leave calling cards that are quite so subtle or persuasive.

It would be foolish to reject the possibility of a genuine contact altogether. As we have seen, there are a few more powerful messages which seem to suggest that there is an intellect at work – not merely a random awareness.

Of course, the evidence for survival rests on more than impressions. Much stronger than messages from mediums may be those cases where people experience things at the moment of death. NDEs are not glimpses of heaven as such, because they tell us only about the final stages of life. But when you add these experiences to visions seen by those who are dying and phenomena witnessed by friends, relatives or medical staff in proximity to them, this suggests that the process is a transition and not a disintegration.

Sceptics will always say that we misread the way the body adjusts to death – its use of our own natural defences and painkillers. But if we are just biological machines, why are such things necessary? If a robot comes to the end of its useful life it switches off. It does not need to have an out-of-body experience, visualise dead loved ones and demonstrate enhanced powers of the mind to ease the passing.

Wishful thinking is the enemy of all who try to probe the supernatural, and it is never more fierce an opponent than when facing up to the question of survival after death. Because so many of us want to believe we tend to be less discriminating than we ought to be. But why do we all find it so hard to disbelieve?

There seem to be two possibilities. The reductionist would argue that it is a defence mechanism to avoid thinking about our own non-existence. But what purpose is served by having developed this delusion if it is not true? Much of the world – from great architecture to the major religions, from every significant humanitarian act to the bloodiest wars – is founded on it. It is hardly irrelevant to human behaviour and, if we are machines responding to the laws of evolution, what good does it do to conjure up such lies?

The other possibility is that we all do have an inner self that is beyond the physical body, and that each of us is intuitively aware of that fact. Indeed, if reincarnation is true (and it makes sense of all the injustice that we see around us, when most religions fail miserably in that regard) then we have all been in heaven many times before. Is that what makes this belief so strong? Do we know it is the truth? Does it explain why so many of us instinctively believe that we do live on?

Some powerful case histories, strong evidence and personally convincing anecdotes favour survival. But these have to be weighed against growing recognition of how the human mind can do things that are truly extraordinary. It will probably always come down to making a choice between visions in the mind and an intuitive awareness of some fundamental truth.

But science now tells us that all reality is created in the mind. Perhaps after death that is what happens. The mind creates a new reality and we simply shift our point of awareness away from the here and now. If that is a delusion, so be it, but it makes undoubted sense to be ready for that possibility should it happen when our time comes. For what do we lose by contemplating heaven? What do we gain by insisting that there is no such thing?

If the critics are right and the here and now is all there is, we should live our lives on the presumption of that possibility. This we can do irrespective of our beliefs. But if – and it is at worst a fifty-fifty possibility – those who profess that there is an afterlife are the ones who are right, then it is a definite advantage to be familiar with what that heaven is supposed to be like.

Being familiar is the first step towards being prepared.

REFERENCES AND FURTHER READING

Much of the material in this book is derived from the authors' own investigations. However, all researchers rely on the work of others and we would like to thank the authors of those sources with which we have not been involved.

Beliefs

The Bible (standard revised edition, Collins, 1952)
Man, Myth and Magic, ed. Richard Cavendish (Purnell, 1970)
Witchcraft: A Strange Conflict, Peter Hough (Lutterworth, 1991)
Powers of Darkness, Powers of Light, John Cornwell (Viking, 1991)

Apparitions

The Oxford Companion to the Mind, ed. Richard Gregory (Oxford University Press, 1987)
Scary Stories, Peter Hough and Jenny Randles (Futura, 1991)
Hutchinson Dictionary of Science, ed. Peter Lafferty and Julian Rowe (Helicon, 1993)
Supernatural Britain, Peter Hough (Piatkus, 1995)
Encyclopedia of the Unexplained Peter Hough and Jenny Randles (Michael O'Mara, 1995)

Point of Death

On Death and Dying, Elisabeth Kübler-Ross (Macmillan, 1969)
Life After Life, Raymond Moody (Bantam, 1976)
At the Hour of Death, Karlis Osis and Erlendur Haraldsson (Avon, 1977)
Life at Death, Kenneth Ring (Coward, McCann and Geoghegan, 1980)
Recollections of Death, Michael Sabom (Harper and Row, 1982)

Heading Towards Omega, Kenneth Ring (Morrow, 1984)
Dying to Live, Susan Blackmore (Grafton, 1993)
Strange but True? Jenny Randles and Peter Hough (Piatkus, 1994)
Saved by the Light, Dannion Brinkley and Paul Perry (Piatkus, 1994)
Parting Visions, Melvin Morse and Paul Perry (Piatkus, 1995)

Reincarnation

Twenty Cases Suggestive of Reincarnation, Dr Ian Stevenson (University of Virginia, 1974)
More Lives than One? Jeffrey Iverson (Pan, 1977)
Mind Out of Time, Ian Wilson (Gollancz, 1981, revised edn Corgi, 1983)
Life Before Birth, Peter and Mary Harrison (Futura, 1983)
The Case for Reincarnation, Joe Fisher (Bantam, 1984)
The Powers of the Mind, Joe Keeton and Simon Petherick (Hale, 1987)
Yesterday's Children, Jenny Cockell (Piatkus, 1993)
Star Children, Jenny Randles (Hale, 1994)
Strange but True? Casebook, Jenny Randles (Piatkus, 1995)

Dreams, Lucid Dreams and Altered States

Out of the Body Experiences, Celia Green (Hamish Hamilton, 1968)
Apparitions, Celia Green and Charles McCreery (Hamish Hamilton, 1975)
The Dream Game, Ann Faraday (Harper and Row, 1976)
Natural History of the Mind, G. Rattray-Taylor (Secker and Warburg, 1979)
Beyond the Body, Sue Blackmore (Heinemann, 1982)
Lucid Dreaming, Stephen LaBerge (Ballantine, 1985)
Far Journeys, Robert Monroe (Souvenir, 1986)

Spiricom and Vidicom

Breakthrough, Konstantin Raudive (Smythe, 1971)
Carry On Talking, Peter Bander (Smythe, 1972)
The Ghost of 29 Megacycles, John Fuller (Grafton, 1987)
After We Die, What Then?, George Meek (Metascience, 1987)

Visitors from Heaven

Gods, Spirits and Cosmic Guardians, Hilary Evans (Aquarian, 1987)
Mary's Message to the World, Annie Kirkwood (Blue Dolphin, 1991)

Mediums

Mediumship and Survival, Alan Gauld (Heinemann, 1982)
A Woman of Spirit, Doris Collins (Grafton, 1986)
Mind to Mind, Betty Shine (Corgi, 1987)
A Psychic Eye, Nella Jones (Ebury Press, 1992)
In Touch with Eternity, Stephen O'Brien (Corgi, 1992)
The Country Beyond, Jane Sherwood (C.W. Daniel, 1992)

Messages from Heaven

On the Edge of the Etheric, Arthur Findlay (Psychic Press, 1945)

The Tibetan Book of the Dead, ed. W. Evans-Wentz (Oxford University Press, 1960)

Life in the World Unseen, Anthony Borgia (Corgi, 1966)

Phone Calls from the Dead, D. Scott Rogo and Raymond Bayless (Prentice-Hall, 1979)

Gateway, Roger Whitby (Psychic Press, 1979)

Guidance by Silver Birch, ed. Anne Dooley (Psychic Press, 1980)

Wisdom from White Eagle, White Eagle Trust (Psychic Press, 1992)

Teachings of Silver Birch, ed. A. W. Austen (Psychic Press, 1993)

Russell, Gwen Byrne (Psychic Press, 1994)

Conversations Beyond the Light, Pat Kubis and Mark Macy (Continuing Life Research, 1995)

General

The Medium, the Mystic and the Physicist, Lawrence Le Shan (Turnstone, 1974)

Stalking the Wild Pendulum, Itzhak Bentov (Dutton, 1977)

Survival?, David Lorimer (Routledge and Kegan Paul, 1984)

Natural and Supernatural, Brian Inglis (Hodder and Stoughton, 1987)

The Afterdeath Experience, Ian Wilson (Sidgwick and Jackson, 1987)

Beyond the Occult, Colin Wilson (Corgi, 1989)

The Afterlife, Jenny Randles and Peter Hough (Piatkus, 1992)

USEFUL ADDRESSES

Regular research and publications into life after death can be found through the following sources. ASSAP (the Association for the Scientific Study of Anomalous Phenomena) investigate spontaneous cases such as hauntings, OOBEs and past life memories. The SPR (Society for Psychical Research) and ASPR (American version) are more concerned with scientific and laboratory work. The sceptical perspective is provided by the two appropriately named magazines. *Psychic News* appears weekly with the latest information from Spiritualist circles. The Noah's Ark Society delve into physical mediumship and materialisation phenomena. *Fortean Times* is a monthly glossy journal that reviews the supernatural in a responsible but lively fashion. *Fate* always has a selection of personal stories of survival after death as told by its readers. *Reincarnation International* is a subscription-only quarterly on this area of research. IANDS (the International Association for Near Death Studies) is the specialist body researching near death experiences and regularly updates this field. Metascience and Continuing Life Research have a similar role with electronic voice, Spiricom and (the latter) with Vidicom research, and offer advice on how to build your own equipment to experiment with instrumental contact with the afterlife.

ASPR   5 West 73rd Street, New York, NY 10023, USA
ASSAP   31 Goodhew Road, Croydon, Surrey, CRO 6QZ, UK
Continuing Life Research   PO Box 11036, Boulder, CO 80301, USA
Fate   PO Box 1940, Future Way, Marion, OH 43305–1940, USA
Fortean Times   PO Box 2409, London NW5 4NP, UK
IANDS   PO Box 193, London SW1K 9JZ, UK
Metascience   PO Box 737, Franklin, NC 28734, USA
Noah's Ark Society   Treetops, Hall Road, Cromer, Norfolk NR27 9JG, UK
Psychic News   Clock Cottage, Stansted Hall, Stansted, Essex CM24 8UD, UK

Reincarnation International   PO Box 26, London WC2H 9LP, UK
The Skeptic   PO Box 475, Manchester, M60 2TH, UK
Skeptical Inquirer   PO Box 229, Buffalo, NY 14215, USA
SPR   49 Marloes Road, London W8 6LA, UK

The authors participate in a network across northern Britain known as NARO (Northern Anomalies Research Association). This produces a journal called *NARO Minded* which covers a range of strange phenomena. They would be very keen to hear from any readers with personal evidence of life after death or the paranormal, which will be treated in confidence if requested. They can be contacted at 6 Silsden Avenue, Lowton, Warrington WA3 1EN, England.

INDEX

ABOUT THE AUTHORS

JENNY RANDLES trained as a science teacher and has a diploma in media communications. She has had a lifelong interest in strange phenomena, tempered by her desire to conduct objective investigations and establish their credibility (or otherwise). She is an honourary life member of BUFORA (British UFO Research Association), which she first joined when at school in 1969. She served as its Director of Investigations for 12 years and since 1989 has scripted and presented the weekly nationwide news and information service, 'UFO Call'. During her time as BUFORA investigations co-ordinator she helped create a Code of Practice, unique in paranormal research. This sets out guidelines to investigators and aims to protect the public from abuse. She was also behind the moratorium, introduced in 1988, that saw BUFORA lead the world by banning the use of regression hypnosis. This is a practice that in her opinion can put the health and psychological welfare of witnesses in jeopardy.

She is also closely associated with several other organisations. In 1982 she was one of the founders – and the original Director of Investigations – with ASSAP (Association for the Scientific Study of Anomalous Phenomena). She is the UK representative and a regular contributor to the prestigious American group, The Dr J Allen Hynek Center for UFO Studies. In addition she is an original member of the Charles Fort Institute, a 25 year long member of NARO (Northern Anomalies Research Association) and has worked with and lectured for the SPR (Society for Psychical Research).

One of her passions is the conducting of large-scale experiments involving hundreds or thousands of people at once. These have tested remote viewing, ESP and precognition through magazines such as *She* and have even included the world's first 'psychic treasure hunt' where people were encouraged to try to dream, or see in visions, the location of a prize as a test of psychic abilities. Her investigations into life after death have included experiments with various mediums, first-hand testing of past life memories and the study of spontaneous cases.

Jenny has written and presented a series of six half-hour documentaries called *Fact or Fiction?* probing various aspects of the paranormal for BBC radio. In April 1996 she wrote and presented her own TV documentary for the BBC making an objective study of the British government's role in UFO sightings. This obtained a record audience figure and generated widespread media attention. In addition Jenny was contracted to be the 'story consultant' in 1993 for the pilot episode of the ITV series *Strange but True?* and served in that officially credited capacity for all four series that followed (1994–1998). She has also worked behind the scenes on numerous other features and documentaries, ranging from a comedy routine with Stan Boardman to a four hour series for the Discovery Channel. She has featured on more than 200 TV series all over the world discussing subjects as diverse as aliens, ghosts, out of body experiences, spontaneous human combustion and real life time travel. Jenny also became Britain's first 'Paranormal Agony Aunt' for the ITV teletext service for several years. Today she regularly answers readers' questions on such matters for the *Daily Mail*.

Jenny Randles has sold one million copies of her investigative books world wide, with editions in more than 20 countries. She has lectured all over the world in locations as varied as prestigious universities such as MIT, the House of Lords and a casino at Surfer's Paradise in Australia. Her articles have appeared in a vast range of sources from tabloids such as the *Weekly News*, magazines like *TV Quick*, leading science periodicals including *New Scientist* and *Omni*, house journals of the police and airlines, and national newspapers *The Times* and the *Guardian*.

PETER HOUGH is an active researcher and field investigator of the unexplained. He is chairman of the Northern Anomalies Research Organisation (NARO), and is a member of the Association for the Scientific Study of Anomalous Phenomena (ASSAP). Peter sees his role as that of a detective, sifting through the facts of a story to determine the truth. Scientific evaluation is available to him through contacts at the University of Manchester Institute of Science and Technology (UMIST). In recent years he has worked with a number of mental health specialists studying people who have suffered UFO abduction experiences.

Peter is author and joint author of fifteen books which have been translated into fourteen different languages, and has published over 200 features for major magazines and newspapers in Britain and abroad. He has lectured extremely widely including to RAF personnel and members of the Institute of Physics. He was one of the first ufologists to lecture in the planetarium at the prestigious Jodrell Bank Telescope Science Centre.

Peter Hough has acted as consultant for many television companies including the BBC, London Weekend Television and Nippon Television in Japan. He was involved in LWT's first series of *Strange But True?* and *Philip Schofield's One in A Million*. Peter has appeared many times on television, has taken part in several documentaries and countless radio programmes.

ALSO AVAILABLE FROM PIATKUS

THE COMPLETE BOOK OF UFOS
Jenny Randles and Peter Hough

What is the truth behind the UFO phenomenon? Who or what is behind it? How much 'evidence' is there – and is it being taken seriously? In the 1990s, UFOs are at last attracting the attention of specialists from all branches of science. Peter Hough and Jenny Randles have unparalleled access to reported sightings and findings all over the world. In this authoritative book, they investigate the extraordinary growth of UFO phenomena and explore the events and major cases that have formed the turning points in UFO history. *The Complete Book of UFOs* offers new insights and includes previously unpublished material from experts and witnesses around the world.

£6.99 PAPERBACK

THE AFTERLIFE
Jenny Randles and Peter Hough

The Afterlife is a fascinating investigation into what happens to us after we die. Should we believe the stories we hear about near-death experiences, out-of-body survival, reincarnation, ghostly hauntings and messages from beyond the grave? Does a part of us live on after death? In this book, Jenny Randles and Peter Hough present an enthralling mixture of scientific facts and spine-chilling stories. This intriguing book will help you to make up your own mind once and for all . . .

£6.99 PAPERBACK

THE PARANORMAL SOURCE BOOK
Jenny Randles

The Paranormal Source Book is a comprehensive guide to strange phenomena from around the world. From ghostly apparitions to crop circles, from spiritual healing to spontaneous combustion, *The Paranormal Source Book* is a fascinating read for anyone interested in all aspects of the paranormal. It offers valuable advice for researchers on methodology and investigation practice, and for those who have witnessed something strange, Jenny Randles advises on what to do and how to deal with any problems that might arise. Phenomena covered include alien abduction, ball lightning, cosmic messages, earth mysteries, ESP, ghosts, ice bombs, near-death experiences, precognition, reincarnation, synchronicity, UFOs, zoological mysteries and much more.

£9.99 PAPERBACK